Effec
Crisis Management

A Robust A-Z Guide for Demonstrating Resilience by Utilizing Best Practices, Case Studies, and Experiences

Sarah Armstrong-Smith

www.bpbonline.com

Group Product Manager: Marianne Conor

Publishing Product Manager: Eva Brawn

Senior Editor: Connell

Content Development Editor: Katherine Schmidt

Technical Editor: Daniel Sparrow

Copy Editor: Joe Austin

Language Support Editor: Justin Baldwin

Project Coordinator: Tyler Horan

Proofreader: Khloe Styles

Indexer: V. Krishnamurthy

Production Designer: Malcolm D'Souza

Marketing Coordinator: Kristen Kramer

First published: 2023

Published by BPB Online
WeWork, 119 Marylebone Road
London NW1 5PU

UK | UAE | INDIA | SINGAPORE

ISBN 978-93-55512-710

www.bpbonline.com

Dedicated to

*My father **Michael**, who taught me the importance of putting people first, and my inspiration for so much of this book.*

*My late mother **Linda**, who taught me that I can be whatever I want to be, and to be fearless in my quest. She would also teach me the true meaning of resilience.*

&

*My partner **David**, who has been by my side every step of the way over the last 20+ years. Always being my rock when I most needed it.*

About the Author

I am **Sarah Armstrong-Smith**. I have had a long and impactful career in business continuity, disaster recovery, cybersecurity, and crisis management, which enables me to operate holistically to understand the threat landscape, and how this can be proactively enabled to deliver effective resilience.

I currently operate as a Chief Security Advisor in Microsoft, and act as an executive sponsor to strategic and major customers across Europe. Prior to joining Microsoft, I worked for several large institutions across the public and private sector, including Thames Water, AXA, EY, Fujitsu, and the London Stock Exchange Group. I have been on the front-line of many major incidents, including IT failures, data breaches, and fraud. I talk passionately about the 'human-aspects' of cyber and building trust and transparency.

I am a Fellow of the British Computer Society and have been recognized as one of the most influential and inspiring people in UK Tech, regularly contributing to thought leadership, industry publications and journals.

I want you to know that as someone who has spent over 25 years working on the strategic, tactical, and operational response to major incidents and crises, I have walked in your shoes, and I know the kind of things that you're potentially dealing with.

From my early days working as Fraud Controller, and Business Continuity Analyst, right through to working as an Executive and Board Advisor, I have come to understand what works well and what doesn't. I embraced each opportunity that came my way, not necessarily knowing where it may lead, but just knowing that it gave me a thirst for knowledge, and a burning desire to deliver positive change.

As you will come to learn in this book, what drives me, and what grounds me is people – every product, every service that is produced by every organization, has to be about benefiting the lives and welfare of people. Because if it isn't – then quite frankly what are we doing, and why are we doing it?

It is often the reality and tragedy of a major incident or crisis, that brings us thumping back down to earth, as a stark reminder of how precious life is.

So, before we go any further, just ask yourself: *what do you stand for, and what motivates you the most?*

Why did I write this book?

Whilst I have seen many books, that provide templates, and best practice on what should be included in an incident response and crisis management plan, rarely I have seen a book that delves behind the scenes and goes that one step further with bringing the organizational and personal experiences together.

Through each of the chapters you will learn something about me and my background, and why and how my career has evolved the way it has, and why I am so passionate about taking a people-centric approach to managing a crisis.

The case studies I have chosen are typically large-scale events that are in the public domain, often coupled with detailed investigation reports and public inquiries, so that you may delve into these, and explore the reports and findings for yourself. It is testament to those people that took the time to document and share such detailed reports, that we can even reflect on these today.

I have shared my own journey, including personal tragedy, to highlight how organizational and emotional resilience in the face of adversity goes hand in hand, and cannot be separated.

Delivering and managing an effective response crisis response is more than just doing the right thing, it drives huge opportunities for stability, growth and innovation within your organization and surrounding communities. Now that has to be a win/win, right?

I hope you enjoy reading this book, as much as I enjoyed writing it.

About the Reviewer

Abbas Kudrati, a long-time cybersecurity practitioner and CISO, is Microsoft Asia's Chief Cybersecurity Advisor. Abbas works with customers on cybersecurity strategy, how Microsoft sees the threat landscape, how we are investing in the future of security at Microsoft, and how organizations can take advantage of Microsoft's security solutions to help improve their security posture and reduce costs.

In addition to his work at Microsoft, he serves as an executive advisor to Deakin University, LaTrobe University, HITRUST ASIA, EC Council ASIA, and many security and technology startups. He supports the broader security community through his work with ISACA chapters and student mentorship. He is also a part-time professor at Deakin University, Melbourne, Australia and a regular speaker on Zero Trust, cybersecurity, cloud security, governance, risk, and compliance.

Abbas has received multiple industry awards, such as "Business Leader/ Professional of the year 2021 by IABCA," "Top Security Advisor for APJ for the year 2020 and the year 2019," "Best Security Professional of the year 2018," "CISO 100 Award 2018," "Finalist for Australian CISO of the year 2015," "IT Governance Professional of the year 2014," and "Security Strategist of the year 2011."

He is the bestselling author of books such as, "Threat Hunting in the Cloud", "Zero Trust Journey Across the Digital Estate", and "Digitization Risks in Post Pandemic World".

He graduated from Gujarat University, India, with a bachelor's degree in Accounting and Auditing and is a certified Forrester Zero Trust Strategist, C I CISO, CISM, CISA, CGEIT, CPDSE, and CSX-P, among other professional certifications.

Acknowledgement

There are a few people I want to thank for the continued and ongoing support they have given me during the writing of this book.

First and foremost, my good friend **Lisa Forte**, 'Partner, Red Goat Cyber Security', for her review and scrutiny of the book, and her valuable feedback. I have huge admiration for Lisa and her work. Not only is Lisa a speaker, trainer, and entrepreneur, but she is also a high-altitude climber and caver, and has a level of grit and determination that is hugely inspiring! Lisa is an expert in running cyber crisis simulations and training higher risk staff on insider threats and social engineering. Having known Lisa for several years, and watched her deliver fascinating keynotes, I knew that Lisa would be the perfect person to review this book, particularly the deep learning from the case studies.

To **Dalim Basu**, 'Chairman, Central & North London Branches of BCS (British Computer Society) – The Chartered Institute for Information Technology' for his kind and supportive demeanor, and his continued faith in me. It was with Dalim's support that I became a Fellow of the BCS in 2021, a role that I'm very passionate about. Dalim has a rich and diverse IT background. He was previously Director of DSL IT Risk Management Consultancy and has worked in the UK and other countries (up to global level) for major firms such as PwC, KPMG, Chase Manhattan Bank, ITN, Lehman Brothers, Lloyds Banking Group, Mitsubishi, Mizuho Bank, Nomura, Shell, and Zurich Financial Services. Dalim is a firm believer in the high value of IT professionalism and actively encourages and promotes it at many levels. He was honored by BCS with the prestigious John Ivinson Award 2022, in recognition of his "truly exceptional voluntary service across a wide range of the Institute's activities".

I am hugely grateful to the wonderful **Nadja El Fertasi**, 'Founder, Thrive with EQ' for her review and support of the book. Nadja and I share a deep passion for people, and her guidance on security culture and emotional intelligence has been gratefully received. Her research and ideas on the human aspects of resilience really helped to bring many aspects of this book to life. Nadja spent two decades working in cybersecurity at NATO, and now runs a consultancy and training business, Thrive with EQ. As the name suggests, she specializes in helping individuals and organizations build resilience by understanding how important emotional intelligence is in managing security risks for humans, both at home and in the workplace.

A huge thank you to my colleagues at Microsoft...

To **Emilia Retta**, 'Senior Director Strategic Resilience and Crisis Response' for her enthusiasm, and thoughtful feedback. When I first told her I was writing the book, she was elated and couldn't wait to read it. With a shared passion for crisis response, and going above and beyond the call of duty, I knew that Emilia would be a great advocate for the book, and her feedback is much appreciated. For over eighteen years, Emilia has served as a global crisis & resilience strategic advisor, providing crisis response, business continuity, and counter-intelligence consulting services to the US intelligence community and various multinational and government clients, including PwC, First Republic Bank, and Deloitte.

For her illustrations on each chapter, **Becky Cholerton**. I have been a fan and admirer of her work, so was over the moon when she agreed to utilize her vision and talent to create inspiring and uplifting images for each chapter. Becky shares a passion for security and compliance.

And last, but no by means least my friend and colleague **Abbas Kudrati**, 'Asia-Pacific Chief Security Advisor, and Technical Editor' for convincing me to put pen to paper and write this book. His support and encouragement have been invaluable in getting the book over the line. Abbas has authored and contributed to several books on threat hunting in the cloud, and zero-trust with more in the pipeline. Abbas is recognized as an award-winning CISO, cloud & cybersecurity strategist, University Professor, as well as an Executive Advisory Board Member, and keynote speaker.

Preface

Today, organizations need simple and practical guidelines that can effectively adapt to the evolving environmental, technological, and social threats. Being resilient is not about stopping each, and every incident, but having a strategy that enables an effective and efficient crisis response, which provides enough flexibility and agility to manage a wide range of major events.

The book's scope is written to appeal to a wide range of readers. From seasoned incident and crisis management responders looking for a refresher, and some top tips, to those who are looking for guidance on how to avoid making costly mistakes.

The reader will be in a better position to strategize, plan and design a credible and defensible incident response and crisis management strategy for their organization, understand the relevance of each subject, learn the best practices from the case studies and personal anecdotes of the author. This will enable a significantly improved crisis response, irrespective of the type of incident. The case studies and personal stories have been specifically chosen to highlight key lessons, and so where applicable only roles in an organization are identified and not specific people.

As shall be discussed further in the book, the aim is to build on the work and observations performed by others, so that we may collectively take action to break the cycle and deliver proactive change.

Each chapter is structured to reflect a letter of the alphabet, and in the words of *Simon Sinek*[1] we need to *"Start with Why"*.

'Why' – Why is this subject important in the context of crisis management response and resilience, and how does it relate to the other chapters in the book

'What' – What are some of the key principles and leading practice that should be considered when it comes to the good, the bad, and the ugly. Wherever necessary I will be highlighting some case studies and anecdotes, which are examples of where some organizations got it right, or wrong, and what we learn from this.

'How' – Practical considerations and actions that can be taken when formulating the strategic and tactical response to a crisis, and how to implement them effectively.

---

1 Simon Sinek, Start with Why: How great leaders inspire others to act, 6 October 2011

Here is a further breakdown of chapter contents, which can also be used as a quick reference guide and reminder of the key subject areas. These are structured as letters of the alphabet to make the key principles easy to remember

A = Action	**N = Near Miss**
B = Believable	**O = Opportunity**
C = Communication	**P = People**
D = Diligence	**Q = Questions**
E = Empathy	**R = Resilience**
F = Fact	**S = Strategy**
G = Gravitas	**T = Time**
H = Honesty	**U = Underdog**
I = Investigation	**V = Victory**
J = Justice	**W = Wellbeing**
K = Knowledge	**X = X (marks the Spot)**
L = Lessons	**Y = Y (pronounced the same as WHY)**
M = Media	**Z = Zero Trust**

I first published a snapshot for each letter during 'Cyber Awareness Month' during October 2021 on LinkedIn. These were my own musings, but it received such a great response, and feedback, that the idea for the book came about, to provide a deeper explanation and guidance on each letter and subject.

The purpose of this book is not to tell you what decisions and actions you should make, as this will be dependent on your organization's risk appetite and overall level of resilience, but to equip you with the knowledge and understanding of what needs to be considered, and why.

The reason I chose an A-Z is because I believe in cutting through complexity and delivering simplicity. The reality is that I want you to remember the **26 letters** and what they stand for in this context. The remainder of the chapters address why these letters are important, and how they relate to each other, as context.

Errata

We take immense pride in our work at BPB Publications and follow best practices to ensure the accuracy of our content to provide with an indulging reading experience to our subscribers. Our readers are our mirrors, and we use their inputs to reflect and improve upon human errors, if any, that may have occurred during the publishing processes involved. To let us maintain the quality and help us reach out to any readers who might be having difficulties due to any unforeseen errors, please write to us at :

errata@bpbonline.com

Your support, suggestions and feedbacks are highly appreciated by the BPB Publications' Family.

Did you know that BPB offers eBook versions of every book published, with PDF and ePub files available? You can upgrade to the eBook version at www.bpbonline.com and as a print book customer, you are entitled to a discount on the eBook copy. Get in touch with us at :

business@bpbonline.com for more details.

At **www.bpbonline.com**, you can also read a collection of free technical articles, sign up for a range of free newsletters, and receive exclusive discounts and offers on BPB books and eBooks.

Piracy

If you come across any illegal copies of our works in any form on the internet, we would be grateful if you would provide us with the location address or website name. Please contact us at **business@bpbonline.com** with a link to the material.

If you are interested in becoming an author

If there is a topic that you have expertise in, and you are interested in either writing or contributing to a book, please visit **www.bpbonline.com**. We have worked with thousands of developers and tech professionals, just like you, to help them share their insights with the global tech community. You can make a general application, apply for a specific hot topic that we are recruiting an author for, or submit your own idea.

Reviews

Please leave a review. Once you have read and used this book, why not leave a review on the site that you purchased it from? Potential readers can then see and use your unbiased opinion to make purchase decisions. We at BPB can understand what you think about our products, and our authors can see your feedback on their book. Thank you!

For more information about BPB, please visit **www.bpbonline.com**.

Table of Contents

1. **Introduction**..1

    Structure..1

    Objectives..2

    Expect the unexpected 2

    Digital disruption 2

    Societal disruption...3

    Breaking down the norms 4

    The difference between an incident and a crisis 4

    Conclusion...5

2. **Action**...7

    Structure..8

    Objectives..8

    Establishing accountability for actions.......................8

    Assigning decision makers to actions.........................9

    Bringing actions to life 9

    Building the action plan..10

    The danger of making assumptions...........................10

    Conclusion...11

        Reflection 12

        Suggested actions..12

3. **Believable**...15

    Structure..16

    Objectives..16

    Establishing believability..16

        Why?...16

    Avoid being in denial 17

Building trust...17

Conclusion..17

    Reflection 18

    Suggested actions..18

4. Communication **19**

Structure..20

Objectives..20

Case study 1...21

Tailoring stakeholder communications 24

When to communicate? 24

Method of communication...25

Who will communicate? 25

Verifying communications 26

Conclusion..27

    Reflection 27

    Suggested actions..27

5. Diligence **29**

Structure..30

Objectives..30

Oversight of risks...31

Establishing a duty of care 31

Diligence in a crisis..32

Tick-boxing for compliance...33

Conclusion..34

    Reflection 34

    Suggested actions..34

6. Empathy **37**

Structure..38

Objectives..38

Perils of victim blaming..38

Demonstrating empathy for people...39

Demonstrating empathy for organizations.............................40

Conclusion...41

Reflection *41*

Suggested actions..*41*

7. Facts..**43**

Structure..44

Objectives..44

The pursuit of truth 45

Misinformation versus disinformation 45

Emerging impact of disinformation campaigns.....................46

Fact checking 48

Digital forensics 49

Conclusion...51

Reflection *51*

Suggested actions..*51*

8. Gravitas **53**

Structure..54

Objectives..54

Leadership and gravitas 54

Demonstrating gravitas 55

Conclusion...56

Reflection *56*

Suggested actions..*56*

9. Honesty..**57**

Structure..58

Objectives..58

Demonstrating integrity 59

Believability versus honesty...59

Dealing with whistleblowing...60

Dealing with grievances 60

Conclusion 61

　Reflection 61

　Suggested actions..61

10. Investigation..**63**

Structure...64

Objectives...64

Co-ordinating the investigation..64

Learning from public inquiries...65

Case study 2..66

Results of investigations 72

Conclusion 73

　Reflection 73

　Suggested actions..73

11. Justice..**75**

Structure...76

Objectives...76

Apportioning blame..76

Dealing with negligence 77

Case study 3..78

Miscarriages of justice..87

Conclusion 87

　Reflection 88

　Suggested actions..88

12. Knowledge...**89**

Structure...90

Objectives...90

Turning knowledge into intelligence.. 90

Case study 4.. 91

Education and awareness... 94

Sharing and collaboration 94

Conclusion.. 96

    Reflection 96

    Suggested actions.. 97

13. Lessons **99**

Structure... 100

Objectives... 100

Utilizing the power of hindsight and foresight.. 100

The fallacy of black swan events 101

Case study 5... 102

Importance of isomorphic learning.. 106

Applying lessons 107

Conclusion 107

    Reflection 108

    Suggested actions.. 108

14. Media **109**

Structure... 110

Objectives... 110

Reliance on the media in a crisis.. 110

Communicating with the media..111

Dealing with censorship 112

Conclusion 113

    Reflection 113

    Suggested actions.. 113

15. Near Miss 115

    Structure 116

    Objectives 116

    A game of chance 116

    Incident containment 117

    What would happen next? 117

    Conclusion 118

        Reflection *118*

        Suggested actions *118*

16. Opportunity 119

    Structure 120

    Objectives 120

    Beyond the comfort zone 120

    A leap of faith 121

    Encountering seismic change 123

    Pivoting into crisis management 125

    Dare to be bold 126

    Turning negatives into positives 127

    Conclusion 127

        Reflections *128*

        Suggested actions *128*

17. People 129

    Structure 130

    Objectives 130

    Nothing is more important than people 130

    People over profit 131

    The unpredictability of people 132

    Conclusion 133

        Reflection *133*

        Suggested actions *133*

18. Questions **135**

Structure 136

Objectives 136

Questions to ask pre-incident 136

Questions to ask during an incident 137

Questions to ask post incident 138

Conclusion 138

Reflection *139*

Suggested actions *139*

19. Resilience **141**

Structure 142

Objectives 142

Future-proofing resilience 142

Embracing a culture of resilience and security 143

Demonstrating organizational resilience 144

Strengthening the resilience of others 146

Conclusion 146

Reflection *147*

Suggested actions *147*

20. Strategy **149**

Structure 150

Objectives 150

Strategy and culture 150

Developing scenarios 151

Exercising the crisis response 152

Conclusion 153

Reflection *153*

Suggested actions *154*

21. Time..**155**

    Structure...156

    Objectives...156

    Time is of the essence 156

    The past 157

    The present 157

    The future...158

    Conclusion 158

        Reflection *159*

        Actions *159*

22. Underdog **161**

    Structure...162

    Objectives...162

    A tale of two companies...162

    Survival of the fittest 163

    Disrupted or disrupter? 163

    Conclusion 164

        Reflection *164*

        Suggested actions...*165*

23. Victory..**167**

    Structure...168

    Objectives...168

    Protecting the castle...168

    Understanding human needs 169

    Positive reinforcement 170

    Conclusion 171

        Reflection *171*

        Suggested actions...*172*

24. Wellbeing 173

    Structure 174

    Objectives 174

    Maintaining wellbeing in a crisis 174

    Managing the stressors 175

    Establishing emotional resilience 176

    Case study 6 176

    Case study 7 178

    Finding your path 181

    Dealing with trauma 181

    Recognizing trauma in others 183

    Conclusion 184

        Reflection 184

        Suggested actions 185

25. X - Marks the Spot 187

    Structure 188

    Objectives 188

    Retracing steps to establish a timeline 188

    Conclusion 189

        Reflection 189

        Suggested actions 189

26. Y-Why 191

    Structure 192

    Objectives 192

    Performing deep analysis 192

    Establishing multiple lines of inquiry 193

    Correlating cause and effect 193

    Conclusion 194

        Reflection 194

        Suggested actions 194

27. Zero Trust **197**

Structure 198

Objectives 198

The principles of zero trust 198

A business perspective on zero trust 199

Crossing the boundary of technology and cybersecurity 200

Conclusion 201

Reflection *201*

Suggested actions *201*

28. Final Thoughts **203**

Index **205-208**

CHAPTER 1
Introduction

Evidence shows that how a significant change or incident is handled is often more important than the incident itself. A major incident on one side of the world can cause far-reaching economic and societal impacts, augmented by the media's actions, and affected communities. The mishandling of an incident can cause share prices to plummet, and a reputation damaged beyond repair.

Structure

In this chapter, I will discuss the following:

- Expect the unexpected
- Digital disruption
- Societal disruption
- Breaking down the norms
- The difference between an incident and a crisis
- What is unique about this book?
- What should you know about the author?
- Why did I write this book?

Objectives

This chapter aims to give a basic introduction to why having an effective crisis response is so important in enabling resilience. As the scope and scale of major incidents increase and the interdependencies between organizations extrapolate, it has never been more important to ensure that incident and crisis responders are equipped with the right skills and knowledge to lead and guide the organization through a crisis, no matter what obstacles may be on the horizon.

The objective of each chapter is to provide a simple yet effective guide that will give the reader practical advice on what to do - before, during, and after a major incident or crisis.

Expect the unexpected

Each year multitudes of analysts and advisors deliver their predictions on global threats. These are consistent themes and warnings of what is on the horizon, often with the power to cause massive disruption on a scale that can shake financial markets and economies, sending governments into turmoil or recession.

The highest probability threats are typically environmental (extreme weather, climate change, or natural disasters) or technological (data fraud, theft, and cyberattacks). At the same time, the highest impact is geopolitical (war and weapons of mass destruction).

Megatrends are not that mega – rising/aging populations, climate change, energy crisis, technology advancements, wealth distribution, and poverty, rising crime, mass migration, and trade conflicts – are things that have been talked about for many years and will continue to feature high on the risk agenda.

Even '*black swan events*' – a metaphor so called because it deviates beyond what is expected, are difficult to predict, and have large-scale consequences – are not that unexpected. Historical black swan events point to the rise of the internet and the *dot. com* crash, as well as the 9/11 terrorist attacks.

Hindsight is a powerful tool, and history shows that we should not only expect the unexpected, but chances are that history will also repeat itself.

Digital disruption

Technology is profoundly changing lives and societal norms. Whether for better or worse, it is the cornerstone of an advanced society and shows no signs of slowing down. Soon it will be virtually impossible to buy goods and services without a digital footprint, especially with each new generation that passes.

The sheer volume of connected devices introduces multiple vulnerabilities from a security and privacy perspective, which further exasperates the technological risks. Research into internet organized crime conducted by EUROPOL[1] highlights that *'critical infrastructure,'* which is essential for the maintenance of vital societal functions, health, safety, security, and economic or social wellbeing of its people, are high-value targets for organized crime, fraud, and attack, as data is bought and sold on darknet markets.

Criminals love to exploit a crisis and have seized the opportunities created by the COVID19 global pandemic. This has led to a significant increase in cybercrime-as-a-service, which includes the large-scale auctioning of personal and organizational data to the highest bidders across multiple jurisdictions.

Any disruption, destruction, or compromise of critical infrastructure has a significant impact within the country and within a broader geographical context, resulting in the inability to maintain and deliver vital functions.

Societal disruption

Even in the aftermath of major disasters, formal investigations and public inquiries often reveal that the warning signs were present months, even years before the event. So many missed opportunities to reduce the probability and mitigate the impact of a disruption.

Despite this, most companies will argue that they have risk, **Business Continuity (BC)**, **Disaster Recovery (DR)**, and cybersecurity, and these disciplines have been in place for many years. Why, then, when a major event occurs, are they not prepared?

The irony is that they will not invoke their BC and DR plans in a major incident; they will not pull the plug on a failing project, and they will not change their strategy because to do so would be too disruptive to the business. Many will even argue that invoking a BC or DR plan is cost prohibitive to the organization, even though the actual cost and detriment can be far worse.

Strategy *Business.com*[2] argues: *"Often it is the fear of disruption that can be more damaging than the actual disruption. People tend to overestimate the power of a threat and underestimate the time they have to respond"*.

---

1   Europol, Internet Organised Crime Assessment Report, 2021: https://www.europol.europa.eu/cms/sites/default/files/documents/internet_organised_crime_threat_assessment_iocta_2021.pdf, retrieved 10 July 2022
2   Paul Leinwand and Cesare Mainardi, Strategy Business.Com (Sept 2017) https://www.strategy-business.com/article/The-Fear-of-Disruption-Can-Be-More-Damaging-than-Actual-Disruption, retrieved 15 July 2022

The recovery phase following a major incident can often be substantial and at great cost, especially in the event of investigations and public inquiries.

They are not equipped to handle disruptive events and still seem surprised when such events occur, even though they have been predicted and talked about for many years.

Breaking down the norms

When broken down into its core components, each organization is fundamentally the same. Whether a large-multinational enterprise or a small business, most organizations will have a vision and a set of core values. At the heart of this is typically the desire to be a responsible business, to change the lives of people for the better, and to make a positive impact on society and the environment. If that truly is the vision of each company, then it is time to embody that vision for the greater good.

A change in mindset and culture is required. This includes removing the notion that '*it will never happen to me,*' '*it is not my problem*' mentality. Events have shown that no organization or community is immune to disruption or failure.

The difference between an incident and a crisis

There is perhaps no more significant test of organizational resilience than when faced with an impending or actual crisis.

A key factor that needs to be considered as part of the overall incident and crisis response is articulating the difference between a major incident and a crisis.

Organizations may use the terms interchangeably, or there may be defined metrics and thresholds for moving from an incident to a declared crisis. The important element is that this will differ for each organization, depending on their overall tolerance and maturity to risk and resilience. It may also be subjective, based on the changing economic, geopolitical, and social climate.

As we shall discuss further in this book, there will be large-scale events that go beyond the containment of the organization, with the power and scale to shift the trajectory of the business on a global scale.

When and how to declare a major incident, or a crisis, is one of the critical items that need to be documented by the incident or crisis professional, irrespective of the plans and strategy that may be deployed.

For this book, and to aid with the understanding of some of the terms, the Business Continuity Institute[3] makes the following differentiation:

- **Incident**: A situation that may be, or could lead to, a disruption, loss, emergency, or crisis.

- **Crisis**: A situation with a high level of uncertainty that disrupts the core activities and / or credibility of an organization and requires urgent action.

One of the key factors which separate a crisis from an incident is the sense of urgency and reputational damage. I shall explore why this can be a determining factor for the ongoing success or failure of the organization within this book.

Conclusion

In this opening chapter, I have explored that anything is plausible, and we should expect the unexpected. This book has been designed to equip you will the skills and knowledge needed to guide your organization through a crisis, no matter what may be on the horizon. This is more than just having an incident response plan; it is about considering all the things that could go wrong and ensuring you are pre-empting and prepared for the obstacles that may get in your way to ensure that you can be resilient in a crisis.

At the end of each chapter, I will ask you to take a minute to reflect and consider how this resonates within your organization, whether you can identify any opportunities to deliver systematic and proactive change through the actions I have suggested, and those you may consider for yourself.

So, let us start as we mean to go on, with the next chapter on '*Action.*'

---

3 The Business Continuity Institute, Good Practice Guidelines 2018 Lite Edition, https://www.theb-ci.org/static/f7e73679-88cc-49e1-bec4c61c1f2d23cc/gpg-lite-2018.pdf (Retrieved 9th August 2022)

CHAPTER 2
Action

A = ACTION

"A man is the sum of his actions, of what he has done, of what he can do, nothing else."

—*Mahatma Gandhi, Indian Social Activist*

In any incident, it's important to take deliberate and decisive action. While it's tempting to wait until you have all the information, the quicker you can act to contain, and recover from the incident- the better. Delays in initiating containment and recovery can cause the incident to spiral, which can lead to unintended consequences.

Some incidents can evolve and escalate very quickly, so you need to be prepared for that. While it may sound like a cliché, *'Time'* really is of the essence in a crisis, and decisions need to be made quickly but also need to be well considered. For once that time has passed, you can never get it back.

Structure

In this chapter, I will discuss the following:

- Establishing accountability for actions

- Assigning decision makers to actions

- Bringing actions to life

- Building the action plan

- The dangers of making assumptions

Objectives

This chapter aims to highlight why careful consideration needs to be given to the actions taken at the outset of a major incident or crisis being declared and why every minute counts when it comes to ensuring that each person understands their role, the actions they must take, along with the consequences of those actions.

I will touch upon the issues that people will be faced with when they lack information and how you can help them to make effective decisions.

Establishing accountability for actions

Establishing accountability early on in a crisis is a critical part of building trust with interested parties.

The timeline and extent of the actions that an organization takes at the outset of a significant incident are a good indicator of how much accountability the organization is taking to contain and resolve the incident as quickly and effectively as possible, irrespective of the root cause and reason for the incident.

Another useful indicator of accountability is that senior representatives of the organization are actively involved in the management and coordination of the incident and show a willingness and desire to allocate appropriate resources to incident and crisis management in preparation for and recovering from a major incident.

An indicator that the organization lacks accountability is deflection, whereby the organization is attempting to evade responsibility and accountability by immediately apportioning blame to another party, despite not having completed an investigation. I share an example of how this can manifest as part of the first case study in *Chapter 4, Communication,* relating to the Deep-Water Horizon explosion, where the CEO used deflection tactics as part of their initial communication with the media.

Another indicator that the organization may not demonstrate accountability is that senior representatives are not actively involved in the incident or are too far removed to be effective. This can mean that other personnel, who may lack skills or experience, are left trying to make decisions on behalf of the organization. I share an example of how this can manifest as part of case study 2, in *Chapter 10, Investigation* relating to the Grenfell Tower fire, where junior personnel were forced to improvise due to the incident commanders being unaware of the true extent of the incident on the ground.

Assigning decision makers to actions

Determining who will make the final decision concerning action is a key consideration in the strategy or plan. Does this require the escalation of a specific person in authority, or does it require a majority decision by an executive committee? Are those people available at separate times of the day, are there delegated authorities that can make decisions in their absence, and to what extent? Company directors may also have legal duties to uphold too.

The clock is ticking, and pressure is likely building from internal and external stakeholders. As noted, each decision has consequences and can lead to further actions that need to be taken. So, while *'Time'* is a critical factor, it should not be the significant factor in the decision, but as more time passes, the expectation of action increases.

Bringing actions to life

Let us take an example of a ransomware cyberattack that has potentially impacted your ability to gain access to the corporate IT network. In the initial stages of an incident, you will not have all the facts. You may not know or appreciate the gravity of the situation – what the attacker has access to, how much damage has been caused to systems, or whether data has been exfiltrated or sold on dark markets. Pressure will be building to act. A key consideration is whether an extortion demand has been made from the attackers and the impact on products and services.

Even a decision to pay or not to pay is an action with consequences, let alone subsequent actions that need to be taken to contain and recover systems and services to a known state.

It is for this reason that a core strategy and action plan must be determined in advance. That core strategy needs to be documented and communicated to all decision-makers. I will discuss some of these dilemmas further in case study 3, in *Chapter 11, Justice,* where we look at the actions taken by *Colonial Pipeline* when they suffered a ransomware attack and the repercussions that unfolded based on the actions that took place in the first few hours on the incident, and the knock-on effect that ensued.

Building the action plan

Consider that the incident you planned for is not the one that will be played out in front of you. Every incident, while similar on paper, is completely different. So having a rigid one size fits all plan, or one that does not have the flexibility to adjust to the evolving situation, will not work effectively.

If the incident does not fit the plan or goes off-piste (and I guarantee it will), people may panic and make ill-informed decisions based on false or misleading information, as they are under pressure to act. I shall further explore this in case study 2, where I examine the consequences of being reliant on out-of-date information and how this led to incorrect information being provided to people during the Grenfell Tower fire

Have a set of 'what if' '*Questions*' and responses, which pre-empt several plausible scenarios, potential actions that can be taken, and the consequences of each. This means that the decision maker(s) has options that can be considered based on the incident and the gravity of the situation as it unfolds.

The danger of making assumptions

Confidence in the validity and viability of the actions can be enabled by removing assumptions and turning these into known facts, which have been communicated and exercised.

Turning back to the ransomware example - simply knowing that there are backups of systems and data available is not going to be sufficient. Confidence in the time it will take to recover fully and when this was last tested will enable the decision maker(s) to make informed decisions.

Every action should be considered from the worst-case scenario. So, without knowing the full facts of the incident, you will need an assume failure/compromise mindset. That means assuming the attacker has thoroughly infiltrated the network, that they have exfiltrated extremely sensitive data, and that this data has been publicly exposed, even if not verified. Therefore, containment and recovery should consider a complete rebuild of the environment, right back to the operating system, because it is potentially the best possible action to regain complete control and evict the attacker.

Fear often leads to procrastination and decision paralysis because of the extent of the unknowns. Conflicting information from different sources can exasperate the situation. The incident and crisis response teams require diversity of thought, and a mix of personalities can make a big difference when dealing with such paralysis. This can often be a mix of bold decision-makers and cautious critics that can provide analytical thinking and reasoning to the situation before and during a crisis. The action plan should pre-empt that at the outset of the incident, there will be many unknowns to deal with, which forms part of the initial incident response.

As highlighted, your actions will be determined based on what you know at the time. You will be missing information, and some information may subsequently be found to be incorrect, or some information you may never receive.

Any assumptions you are making in your plan, which are not known facts, should be treated as a risk. Expect an extensive list of those in your risk register to prioritize and fix! While it may seem that there are a lot of unknowns, the more of these that can be closed, the more confidence can be gained.

Your objective is to turn those assumptions into facts, or to highlight that the information is not verified, to ensure the decision maker(s) understands the rationale and basis for the action that may or may not be taken and what is required to increase the confidence in the decision and subsequent outcome. We shall circle back to this subject when we discuss it in *Chapter 7, Facts*.

Conclusion

In this chapter, I have explored why taking deliberate and decisive action is important at the outset of a major incident or crisis. We discussed the difference between no action and inaction and that time should be used wisely. For once it has gone, you can never get it back. Every action or inaction has consequences, and people must be able to fully consider the outcome of their actions and how this will contribute to the overall resolution of the incident.

Reflection

- Consider the organization's current stance and approach to taking action as quickly and efficiently as possible in the event of a major incident or crisis.

- Does the current approach enable you to articulate how the company is demonstrating accountability throughout the lifecycle of the incident?

- Do your actions speak louder than words?

Suggested actions

- Document a clear set of actions that must be taken at the outset of a major incident or crisis, including declaration and escalation.

- List actions in chronological order and highlight those that are mandatory versus recommended. Highlight actions that may depend on previous actions and whether any can be run in parallel.

- State how much time it takes to execute the action, where applicable, and whether the action is part of the critical timeline in terms of the overall objective.

- Each action needs an owner and should highlight whether additional authorization may be required to enact the action and how this shall be achieved. Consider whether pre-approval can be granted to expedite key decisions and approvals.

- Avoid assigning specific names to actions, as this can be compounded if the person is not available. It is better to assign roles to actions and ensure more than one person is assigned or empowered to move into that role in an emergency.

- Consider whether a decision tree may be applicable for some actions, for example, whether certain criteria or information is needed. Provide details on obtaining additional information and potential consequences if an action is made or not made. This enables the action owner to make an informed decision or to escalate where actions cannot be performed or will be delayed.

- If not now, then when? If there is not enough information, or the action needs to be deferred or delayed, what is the impact? For example, other actions cannot start, or they will cause a risk to safety or security. This enables the action owner to assess the circumstances and whether they need to continue to delay or override a previous decision because of the consequences.

- The action owner needs to know what is expected of them regarding their level of authority and empowerment. Every action or inaction has a consequence, so the action owner(s) needs to be aware of the subsequent actions and dependencies placed upon them so that they are prepared if the incident takes a different trajectory than expected.

- It is essential to document the core actions in a plan, checklist, or playbook so that nothing is missed or forgotten. For more complex organizations, this may require an application to assign, and time stamp each action to various parties. Irrespective of how actions are captured and recorded, it is important to try and identify the critical path, so time and resources are not wasted on non-urgent or non-critical tasks. This can also help to identify where resources can be diverted. This does not mean that other actions are not necessary or are no longer required. It means that focus can be given to priority areas as needed.

- Some of the actions may be automatically generated through IT systems, such as taking evasive action to quarantine a device that may have malware detected right through to shutting down internet banking services for consumers. You need to know what actions may be automated and ensure people are prepared for when and how an automated response is triggered. Automation may continue, even if a subsequent decision was made to stop or delay the action. Consider how automated system actions can be controlled and reversed and how they are communicated.

- Each action needs to be recorded - who did what, when, and why? This is required for any subsequent *'Investigation'* or review. The why is important because your decision and the action you take are based on the information available to you at the time. That may turn out to be wrong or flawed, hence the recording of the action as to why you did what you did. If the incident results in injuries, or fatalities, it is likely that this will also entail a public inquiry, regardless of whether this was directly or indirectly caused by the incident.

- All actions should be reviewed post-incident to look for *'Opportunities'* for improvement and *'Lessons'* learned. The aim is to provide a factual account of the events leading up to, during, and after the incident, without prejudice or preconceived ideas on who to blame.

In the next chapter, *'Believable'*, I shall discuss why it is important to demonstrate believability and credibility, with all interested parties.

CHAPTER 3
Believable

B = BELIEVABLE

"To be persuasive, we must be believable. To be believable, we must be credible. To be credible, we must be truthful."

—*Edward. R. Murrow, American Broadcast Journalist*

How many times have you read a company press statement following a significant incident or watched someone speak at a news conference, and though they are saying the right words, you just do not believe what they are saying?

This can be especially true during major incidents.

Structure

In this chapter, I will discuss the following:

- Establishing believability

- Avoid being in denial

- Building trust

Objectives

As well as taking decisive action as early as possible during a major incident, there is a need to consider how to demonstrate trust and transparency. To do this, the messages that people hear must be convincing, which is why I shall discuss the issue of *believability* in this chapter. In particular, our objective is not to start from the point of denial but to be as open as possible.

Establishing believability

What you say is just as important as how you say it. Think about the words and language you use. Think about the message and how this may be construed by various parties.

People will ultimately believe what they can see, feel, and touch more than what is written. The emotional intensity and integrity behind the message will drive people to believe or disbelieve what is happening around them. Perception is, therefore, key. As I shall discuss more in the book, some will also try and manipulate and deceive people into believing a specific narrative.

Anything that starts with *'We take your security/safety very seriously'* when talking about a cyberattack, accident, or data breach normally turns people off because it lacks sincerity and *'Empathy.'*

Why?

Because you are telling people what you think they want to hear, not what is going on. Individuals and other organizations will expect you to take security and privacy seriously. That should be a given.

It can often be perceived as empty words and slightly condescending, even if your intent is well-placed.

Be careful about the message you want to portray and how people will respond, and whether there is even a mechanism to respond.

Your message should be specific to the incident, delivered with *'Gravitas'* and with some humility and grace if people have suffered loss or injury.

Avoid being in denial

Often in the case of a cyberattack or data breach, organizations may be in a position of denial that the company has been the victim of an attack or has fallen foul of a scam. It is, therefore, essential to note just that – the organization is a victim of a crime and should be treated as such.

When we start from a position of denial, where we are consciously trying to deceive the interested parties, this can be an exceedingly tricky position to return to, as this requires having to undo or explain earlier statements. There is a tendency to get embroiled in a web of lies that can be difficult to backtrack from without admitting the deliberate plan to deny that there has been an incident or downplay the severity of the incident.

As I highlighted in the previous chapter, it is crucial to have an *'assume compromise'* mindset, and from a resilience perspective, this can also extend to *'assume failure'* – what can go wrong, will go wrong. It is essential to acknowledge, therefore, that every organization is susceptible to compromise, or failure and mistakes can happen. And as I have highlighted in the introduction, how the organization handles a compromise and failure is essential.

Building trust

So, the first objective is to be upfront about the fact that you have had an incident and to have a firm strategy that intends to be as open and transparent as possible from day 1. In the next chapter, we discuss the importance of establishing credibility with *'Communication,'* I state how to deliver this in *Chapter 8, Gravitas.*

The underpinning need is to establish and maintain trust in the organization as early as possible in the incident, which is an essential element of brand protection. How believable you are during and after a crisis plays a large part in how key stakeholders perceive their trust in you and whether they think you demonstrate *Honesty.*

Conclusion

In this chapter, I have explored why there is a need to demonstrate trust and transparency as early as possible and why we must be believable. Starting from a position of denial does little to demonstrate trust and will cause more issues down the line if it becomes apparent that the organization deliberately withheld information.

Reflection

- Consider the approach to crisis management within your organization and whether it is clear what your overall intent is when faced with a major incident or crisis.

- Are you fostering an open and transparent environment to engender trust in the organization?

- How will you establish and promote credibility in what you say and do?

- Does this have top-down support and commitment from senior management, and are they actively engaged in all aspects of the crisis management and resilience strategy?

Suggested actions

- Create a clear mission statement and vision for the incident and crisis management strategy. Consider how key principles for effective crisis response can be included in the vision and whether it is driving the proper outcomes.

I have established in this chapter that what you say is just as important as how you say it. Think about the message and how this may be construed by various parties. In the next chapter, I shall bring this to life by profoundly diving into the effectiveness of 'Communication'. I shall also look at what happens when things go wrong as we look at the first case study.

CHAPTER 4
Communication

C = COMMUNICATION

"The single biggest problem in communication is the illusion that it has taken place."

—*George Bernard Shaw, Irish playwright, and critic*

It sounds obvious, but communication is so crucial during each stage of a major incident.

This is important, so I'll repeat it: *communicate, communicate, communicate!*

Your communication needs to be clear, concise, and credible.

You need to consider who your key stakeholders are, what are THEIR needs and expectations, how they will be communicated with, and when. Also, who will deliver the communication?

I have highlighted 'THEIR' in capitals as this is a critical aspect of effective communication. All too often, we think about what we want to communicate, why this is beneficial to us, and what we will get out of it. But, unless we are considering communication through the lens of the person that is the subject of the communication, how can we expect people to act or to care about the incident or your organization? You need to take action to listen and understand before you can hope to be understood.

Structure

In this chapter, I will discuss the following:

- Case Study 1: B.P. Deep Water Horizon

- Tailoring stakeholder communications

- When to communicate

- What to communicate

- Method of communication

- Who will communicate

- Verifying communications

Objectives

In this chapter, I will discuss the importance of effective and timely communication. This needs to be performed from the outset of the incident, right through to the conclusion. We will explore why different stakeholders have varying expectations regarding the type of communication they receive and who will provide it. In addition, we shall take a look at our first case study, where we will see the impact of what happens when communication is handled poorly and the consequences this can have for the organization.

Case study 1

Let us look at the first case study, which relates to the B.P. Deepwater Horizon oil spill in April 2010. Despite it being acknowledged that this event was one of the worst ecological and marine disasters in U.S. History, what we can observe is the comments made to the '*Media*' by the *Chief Executive Officer* (*CEO*) within the first few weeks of the tragedy:

Case Study 1
B.P. Deepwater Horizon Oil Spill
The Gulf of Mexico, 2010
Summary of Incident

On 20 April 2010, the Deepwater Horizon oil rig exploded off the Gulf Coast, killing eleven people and injuring seventeen.

For 87-days, 3.19 million barrels of crude oil spewed into the ocean, which devastated the local ecosystem as thousands of fish, birds, turtles, and dolphins perished. According to the U.S. Environment Agency, this was the most significant environmental disaster in U.S. history, and what ensued was a six-year legal battle to seek justice for those people killed and injured and the ecological damage.

In November 2012, B.P. pleaded guilty to felony manslaughter, environmental crimes, and obstruction of Congress. The Assistant Attorney General highlighted[1] that "*The explosion of the rig was a disaster that resulted from B.P.'s culture of privileging profit over prudence.*"

In addition to the resolution of charges against B.P. – the highest-ranking B.P. supervisors onboard the Deepwater Horizon, known as 'well site leaders', engaged in negligent and grossly negligent conduct. According to court documents, the two supervisors indicated that oil and gas were flowing into the well. Despite this, the leaders chose not to take obvious and appropriate steps to prevent the blowout. As a result of their conduct, control of the well was lost, resulting in catastrophe.

In April 2016, the U.S. Department of Justice issued a consent decree[2] levying multiple fines on B.P. under the Clean Water Act, resulting in the largest criminal penalty with a single entity in the U.S., totaling $20.4 billion.

While other organizations were also found culpable for the disaster, this case study centers on how B.P. responded to the initial event.

1 *United States Department of Justice, 15 November 2012:* https://www.justice.gov/opa/pr/bp-exploration-and-production-inc-agrees-plead-guilty-felony-manslaughter-environmental *(retrieved 9 July 2022)*

2 U.S Department of Justice, Deepwater Horizon, 4 April 2006, https://www.justice.gov/enrd/deepwater-horizon (retrieved 10 July 2022)

Comments made in response to the incident

In response to the initial disaster and events, the CEO made multiple media statements[3] to various news outlets around the world over a period of several days and weeks, some of which are summarized as follows by the Guardian newspaper highlighting 'B.P.'s gaffes':

3 May 2010

Less than two weeks after the explosion on the Deepwater Horizon, B.P. chief executive tells the BBC that while it is *"absolutely responsible"* for cleaning up the spill, the company is not to blame for the accident which sank the rig.

"This was not our accident … This was not our drilling rig … This was Transocean's rig. Their systems. Their people. Their equipment."

14 May 2010

The CEO makes his first ill-judged comment when he tells the Guardian that *"the Gulf of Mexico is a vast ocean. The volume of oil and dispersant we are putting into it is tiny concerning the total water volume"*.

Asked if he felt his job was already under threat: *"I don't at the moment. That, of course, may change. I will be judged by the nature of the response."*

30 May 2010

The CEO's most dangerous comments came before a mass of reporters gathering on the Louisiana shore: *"The first thing to say is I'm sorry. We're sorry for the massive disruption it's caused their lives. No one wants this over more than I do. I would like my life back."*

3 June 2010

The Financial Times published an interview with the CEO in which he admits B.P. was unprepared for an oil spill at such depths: *"We did not have the tools you would want in your toolkit."*

---

3   Richard Wray, The Guardian, July 2010, https://www.theguardian.com/business/2010/jul/27/deepwater-horizon-oil-spill-bp-gaffes, (retrieved 19 July 2022)

Analysis of the incident

- What we can identify from the outset of the incident was how the CEO lacked empathy for those most impacted by the tragedy. Empathy requires consciously being sensitive to someone else's needs and feelings. This is an important area that I will explore further in *Chapter 6, Empathy*.

- Within the first 2 weeks of the incident, the CEO had already deflected all blame from the organization and had positioned it at the partners, even though there had been no '*Investigation*' to determine the '*Facts*' at this point.

- The comment on 30 May 2010 was particularly damming, as the CEO showed a callous disregard for the loss of life, and injury that had occurred, even if this was not the intent. The insinuation that this had a higher impact on the life of the CEO rather than on families and loved ones did not go unnoticed by the media and prosecutors. While the CEO attempted to apologize[4] for his actions and comments just a few days later, the damage had already been done, which contributed to the subsequent level of distrust in the organization.

- The overall tone of the statements is aggressive in nature and offers no commitment by the organization to accept accountability to provide '*Diligence*' and learn '*Lessons*.'

Lessons we can learn from this

- What you say is just as important as how you say it.

- Be careful not to make hasty statements that are fueled with emotion. While apologies can be made to try and redact earlier statements, the damage has already been done and will be recorded and utilized in any subsequent '*Investigation*.'

- There is no mention of the people who lost their lives in the communications. I will explain why people are the most critical priority in any incident – without exception, during *Chapter 17, 'People'*.

- While many factors contributed to the Deep-Water Horizon explosion and oil spill, prosecutors highlighted a systematic issue with culture, and multiple failings by the organization, that no doubt contributed to the drawn-out legal battle and record-breaking fines.

- This tragedy would cause long-lasting reputational and financial damage to the organization. On top of the fines levied, B.P. subsequently committed tens of billions of dollars over multiple years to clean the environment and compensate victims

---

4 The HuffPost, 2 June 2010: https://www.huffpost.com/entry/bp-ceo-tony-hayward-apologizes-life-back_n_597966 (retrieved 19 July 2022)

Tailoring stakeholder communications

Communication needs to be relevant and tailored to your audience and what they are interested in; otherwise, you are just speaking into the void. As I discussed in the last chapter, managing people's perceptions and expectations in times of crisis are essential. People see the world as they are, not as it is, since different people and communities have a separate map of the world and experiences.

Be careful about who is writing or signing off the communication.

While it is crucial to ensure that communications are reviewed for accuracy before they are released, too much 'red pen' from the legal department in an attempt to avoid subsequent claims of negligence or blame can mean that the communication is devoid of any emotion, and is nothing more than a bland statement, that leaves the audience asking more questions. This is a core principle of empathy, which I shall explore further in *Chapter 6, "Empathy."*

Any communication strategy and plan must include your employees, who should be regarded as your biggest advocate. I have often seen carefully crafted communications from marketing aimed at customers or the media, but communication has not been provided to employees. This can leave employees feeling despondent and confused, and they are more likely to speculate or try and validate what is happening from external or third-party sources, which adds to the problem.

When to communicate?

Remember that providing some communication is better than no communication at all.

There is often a tendency to want to wait until you have more facts or to see how bad the incident might get before issuing a statement or communication. I have often been on crisis response calls, where the decision criteria went something like this: *"Let us wait 30mins.... then 1 hour... then just one more hour... then wait until after lunch... or wait until X person is on the phone, or country comes online."*

State what you know to be true at the time. Provide a commitment to share more information when it is available, but do not try to make factual statements about what you cannot confirm or where you are not able to verify as accurate. When such statements are later confirmed as incorrect or misleading, it can lead to more questions about how the organization is dealing with the situation. Avoid simply stating *"I don't know"* when faced with a question you cannot answer, as it can also imply a lack of control.

Remember what I said about the ticking clock and needing to make decisions? We shall discuss more crucial factors to consider when it comes to *Chapter 21, 'Time',* for the more time wasted, the less '*Opportunity*' you have to control the narrative and the outcome.

This should include thresholds, triggers for escalation and communication, and the methods. If the primary communication method, such as corporate websites or email, is unavailable, then backup communication forms should be available.

With the '*assume compromise*' mindset, it is necessary to consider the non-availability of the prime communication channel, such as email. We shall discuss more the criticality of communication channels in *Chapter 12, 'Knowledge'*, and the case study on tactics used by the enemy to destroy communications as one of the first objectives when operating in a hybrid war.

Method of communication

When determining the audience of the communication, consider the method, such as written statements, as well as the use of audio and visual statements from accessibility, societal, and cultural perspectives. Given the speed at which news travels, prepare to issue statements at all times of day and in different languages if necessary. This is especially relevant for companies operating or delivering services across multiple countries and time zones. When considering how communication may be translated from one language to another, ensure that key messages remain in context and actions are stipulated in a meaningful way to the recipient. Simply relying on a translation application will not be sufficient, as translations may not be correct or can add to the confusion if the messages are conflicting. It is also prudent to ensure that language is inclusive.

A key consideration is how people like to consume and receive information and communication. For example, not all people have access to digital services and may want or expect to be able to speak to someone directly, either by telephone or in person. The communication strategy should consider the different methods of communication required and how they will be managed, considering each method's benefits and potential issues. For example, a letter will take much longer to arrive than an email.

This is not a one-off; you need to think about how often you will communicate and when people can expect an update. It is acceptable and expected that you would issue a holding statement, but this should only be considered temporary, and this will be followed up with a further statement as quickly as possible.

Who will communicate?

It is necessary to consider who will communicate with each interested party and group of stakeholders.

Will certain parties expect to receive personal communication, or is generic communication acceptable? Consider that an email or letter not signed by a specific person in the organization may leave people feeling despondent. So, in the same way, you need to tailor communications for the audience, you will also need to tailor who will provide the communication and whether it is at an appropriate level.

As I shall discuss further in *Chapter 8, 'Gravitas'*, the most senior person in the organization or department, may not always be the most appropriate person to deliver difficult communications and statements. However, such individuals will be expected to retain accountability for the overall management of the incident or crisis.

People tend to resonate more with those that act and resemble them and whom they like. Utilizing existing and trusted relationships can help to build rapport with those affected.

Another key factor to consider is how you will communicate with the media and who will deliver this. While you may have an objective to try and keep the incident out of the public domain, you should consider that things will inevitably become public as more interested parties become aware of the situation, especially if you have not effectively briefed employees. So, rather than avoiding communicating with the media, this should form part of the overall strategy and plan. We shall discuss these principles further in *Chapter 14, Media*.

Verifying communications

It is not enough to just communicate one way. You will need to check that the relevant parties have received and understood it, especially if you expect the recipient of the communication to take some affirmative action. Simply communicating louder does not mean you have been heard! Similarly, some of your communication can be taken out of context or misquoted. Therefore, clear communications and statements are required, as well as where previous communications can be located.

Do not over-promise and under-deliver by saying you will provide an update every hour if you cannot do this, as it is frustrating for those left waiting and wondering. Similarly, do not state that you will get back to them next week if there is an expectation of a more expedient update.

Finally, for this chapter, it is necessary to also communicate when the incident is over and closed. Depending on the scale of the incident there can be a lot of activity at the outset, but as the incident progresses into containment, recovery, and restoration, which could take weeks or even months.

As we shall identify with some of the case studies, the results of public inquiries can also take years to come to fruition; hence, communications may need to stay active for some time.

While communications may get less frequent, this does not mean they just stop. Acknowledging that the incident has formally closed and a summary of the outcomes and learning points offers additional assurance to the interested parties that the incident has been dealt with and managed effectively.

Conclusion

In this chapter, I have discussed the importance of effective and timely communication. In the first case study, we also explored what can go wrong when communication is mishandled and how this can have a negative impact on the overall crisis response. It is, therefore, important that care is taken not just of what is communicated but also of who will perform the communication and whether they are believable, just like we explored in the previous chapter.

Reflection

- What was your impression of the case study, and how did it make you feel when you read some of the statements in response to the initial communications issued to the media? What would you have done differently?

- Consider your organization's overall stance and approach to internal and external communication. Are you fostering a culture that allows for clear, concise, and transparent communications during a major incident and crisis?

- Have you identified areas where communications have lacked credibility and conviction, and what can you learn from this?

- Are there examples of good or bad communications issued by the organization, or other third parties, that can be used as examples to promote awareness?

Suggested actions

- Create a clear communication strategy and plan for all internal and external interested parties. Ensure that the strategy is inclusive, not exclusive.

- For each interested party, document their needs and expectations and when and how they will receive a communication(s).

- Determine who will communicate with interested parties and whether this needs to be a specific role or person within the organization—for example, public relations personnel for dealing with the '*Media*'.

- Consider the role of communication managers, with delegated authority for creating and authorizing communications. To ensure consistency, what level of empowerment is provided for formal versus informal communications?

- Consider whether specific parties expect to receive personal and tailored communications rather than a generic statement and how this will be delivered. This needs to be evidenced and recorded in the same way as other communications.

- For all parties, identify the mechanism by which they can ask questions or provide feedback. Do not assume that people have understood the communication just because it has been published on a website or released as a statement.

- Set up internal and external communications bureau as a central point of contact for incoming and outgoing communications. This should include a mechanism for employees to ask questions and get support.

- Just like actions, all communications should be recorded and date-stamped for inclusion in the post-incident review and subsequent '*Investigation.*'

In the next chapter, we shall explore the subject of '*Diligence*' and ensuring there is a duty of care when demonstrating accountability during a major incident. This is another important factor when managing stakeholder expectations.

CHAPTER 5
Diligence

D = DILIGENCE

"There is no barrier to success which diligence and perseverance cannot hurdle."

—*Oscar Micheaux, U.S. Filmmaker*

This is about getting a good understanding and appreciation for what could go wrong as a measure of your *'Resilience'* and overall exposure to risk and vulnerabilities.

Your understanding of the changing threat landscape, business model, supply chain, technical assets, and regulatory and compliance requirements will enable you to review and pivot your *'Strategy,'* determine where the gaps are and make informed decisions.

This correlation means you can take pragmatic and proactive steps to increase your preparedness.

This is more than updating and reporting on a risk register; it is being mindful of how the risk could manifest and taking meaningful action to prioritize this.

In addition, there may be requirements to aggregate and consolidate multiple risks to provide a big-picture view. Often, people from different departments will have varying levels of responsibility and accountability and may lack visibility of other threats that have been reported and the upstream and downstream reporting and dependencies that exist. As shall in some case studies, there are challenges when sharing information across departments or entities.

Structure

In this chapter, I will discuss the following-

- Oversight of risks
- Establishing a duty of care
- Diligence in a crisis
- Tick-boxing for compliance

Objectives

This chapter explains why diligence and providing a duty of care are essential from the outset of a major incident. This helps to build and maintain trust, as it demonstrates to interested parties that the organization is going beyond a minimum level of compliance and shows that the company is intent on doing the right thing for the right reasons.

To do this effectively requires a good understanding and knowledge of the type of risks the organization may face and how these could manifest.

Oversight of risks

I have often found that collating and reporting on related subjects can help management understand the full extent of the risk or combination of threats, rather than reporting in siloes or from different parts of the organization.

As an incident and crisis responder, it is prudent to have oversight and visibility of reported risks from different areas of the organization to see if the same issues are being reported or there is correlation between risks that could extrapolate the problem further, if not resolved.

In case study 5, mentioned in *Chapter 13, Lessons*, I shall explore how a lack of sharing, and correlation of information from different sources, led to multiple gaps in intelligence regarding the events that led up to, and contributed to the 9/11 terrorist attacks.

Establishing a duty of care

For many organizations delivering critical services such as healthcare, energy, or food distribution, there is an expectation that the organization has performed appropriate due diligence and taken reasonable care in ensuring the safety, reliability and security of their products and services. This could include taking measures to enable effective product recall if the product fails to meet regulatory or organizational standards, or when there is an actual, or perceived risk to the health and '*Wellbeing*' of people.

The danger can occur when the organization assesses the cost of recall, versus cost of compensation, as just an arbitrary financial number, as opposed to considering the full extent of the situation, and impact. The organization may determine that it is more cost effective to pay people who may be sick or injured because of a faulty or unfit product, rather than bear the cost of removing and replacing the goods or service. The latter means that the organization also must take accountability for producing a defective product, should they decide to perform a recall.

A prime example of where two organizations got it wrong was in the case of Bridgestone, and the Ford Motor Company. Both entities failed to take appropriate and timely action to recall the Ford Explorer, and other similar Sports Utility Vehicles, following an unusually high number of crashes and fatalities, in the early 1990's.

A series of investigations highlighted that defective Firestone tires (approximately 14.4 million), manufactured by Bridgestone, and installed on specific Ford vehicles had contributed to 271 deaths and over 800 injuries in the U.S., and more internationally. The vehicles would suffer tire separations or blowouts, leading to crashes, or vehicles overturning.

In October 2001, the U.S. Department of Transportation, issued a report[1] citing many issues with the failure of both organizations to take appropriate action in recalling vehicles and issuing compensation. In addition, both organizations had potentially downplayed the severity of the defects, and level of recalls that may be required to consumers and in press releases. The report highlighted that the organizations were aware as early as 1996 of the defects and high number of accidents, but recalls did not occur on a large scale until several years later.

Both organizations would publicly blame each other for either the design of the tires, or design of the vehicle, and ineffective information sharing between both parties, which would ultimately lead to the end of a 100-year partnership.

A *University of Illinois Chicago* (UIC) law review[2] conducted in 2004, highlighted that the overall cost to Bridgestone/Firestone was $1.67 billion and Ford Motor Company $530 million. Bridgestone's market price dropped by 50% and the resulting restructuring cost Bridgestone $2 billion. In 2001, Ford recorded a loss of $5.5 billion.

This example of a failure to provide a duty of care, not only demonstrates issues with establishing and accepting accountability early on, but how the true cost of an incident can spiral beyond the initial recall, due to the multiple lawsuits, fines and claims for compensation that ensued. The resulting public inquiries and lack of consumer confidence in the products and organizations can also significantly impact market value for many years. Some organizations may also never recover.

Diligence in a crisis

The expected level of duty of care and diligence continues before, during and after an incident. This provides a deeper understanding of WHY and HOW an incident occurred. The more we can learn lessons, the more we can improve! Lessons are not just part of the post incident review, but are an ongoing iterative process, which takes proactive steps to improve every aspect of the response.

During *Chapter 2, Actions,* I spoke about the importance of verifying any assumptions that are being made in the incident and crisis management plan, and anything that is not a known '*Fact*' should be treated as a risk. In addition, I discussed that there is a difference between making an informed decision, to take no action versus taking no action at all.

---

1 U.S. Department of Transportation National Highway Traffic Safety Administration Safety Assurance Office of Defects Investigation, Engineering Analysis Report, and Initial Decision Regarding EA00-023: Firestone Wilderness AT Tires, October 2021: https://www.nhtsa.gov/sites/nhtsa.gov/files/firestonereport.pdf (retrieved 15th August 2022)

2 Kevin M. McDonald, Separations, Blow-outs, and Fallout: A Treatise on the Regulatory Aftermath of the Ford-Firestone Tire Recall, 37 J. Marshall L. Rev. 1037 (2004), UIC Law Review, https://repository.law.uic.edu/lawreview/vol37/iss4/2/ (retrieved 15th August 2022)

The ability to systematically remove assumptions, to provide clarity on the decisions and actions that need to be made, are core principles of diligence.

Tick-boxing for compliance

Another related principle of diligence is one of compliance– or more specifically *'tick boxing for compliance'* often categorized by doing the minimum amount necessary to achieve a control or objective, potentially needed to satisfy a policy or regulatory requirement.

This can quite often be indicative of a culture that is potentially less focused on diligence.

When working with various organizations on their business continuity and crisis management strategies, I have invariably found there is a significant difference between *'need and want'* - those organizations that do the minimum necessary because they need to, versus those that go the extra mile because they want to.

There are those that may be restricted in the level of diligence that can be performed, due to resource constraints, or other reasons, but this will invariably be acknowledged as a risk by the organization, and they will actively seek to manage, or escalate the risk.

Those with a poor history of diligence, and minimum controls may be more likely to ignore, or delay the fix and closure of safety findings, test, and audit reports. These organizations are potentially more likely to have *'Near Misses'* or not sufficiently learn *'Lessons'* from incidents.

Those with a good history of diligence, often have an ardent desire to understand and get to the truth, show a willingness and desire to explore things that are difficult for some organizations to comprehend, such as highlighting failings by management, acting sooner, or taking appropriate corrective action once identified.

As I shall discuss further in *Chapter 23, Victory*, there is a need to cultivate a culture of psychological safety, that enables people to come forward early on, and seek help. This unfortunately happens too little because of the fear, shame, or guilt that people are made to feel.

I am uneasy with the principle of apportioning blame to people unless there has been a deliberate and willful act of deception, but I think it is an important point to reflect on here. This is another key point that I will reflect on in *Chapter 6, 'Empathy'*.

While there are certainly instances of human error, when analyzed more deeply it is often the organization's culture that has enabled these failings in process to occur. Certainly, a contributing factor is how the organizational culture has developed over time, where actions become embedded as norms. Rarely is it the result of a single person.

Behavior is typically learned and passed down through the organization. For example, if organizations tend to favor the quick and easy route to show compliance, then the culture replicates this behavior as the norm. The same can be said for those that take the time to check and verify and perform sufficient diligence through each stage of the product and service lifecycle.

This is an area we will explore further towards the end of the book, where we examine the root cause of an incident in *Chapters 25* and *26*, where we get to reflect on '*Why*' incidents manifest in the way they do.

Conclusion

In this chapter, I explored why it is important for organizations to demonstrate diligence and a duty of care when dealing with a major incident. Suppose the organization retains control of the incident, such as in the event of a product recall. In that case, it is important for the organization to take early and pragmatic '*Action*' to reduce the impact and accept accountability for the consequences.

Reflection

- Consider the products and services produced by your organization and the expectations and due care expected because of regulatory or organizational standards, measured the experience and expectations of consumers.

- Could a defect in the product or service lead to concerns over safety, reliability of security, and does the organization have an effective incident, and crisis response to manage this?

- Do you provide products and services directly to consumers, or do you provide products and services to other organizations that may rely on your components and parts? What is your contractual commitment and duty of care for ensuring they receive accurate and timely information should issues be encountered?

- Are you performing the minimum level of diligence and compliance expected, or are you going above and beyond the call of duty to be the benchmark that others follow or aspire to?

Suggested actions

- Thinking back to the action plan I discussed in *Chapter 2, Actions,* include the criteria and thresholds for determining what to do when a product or service is proven to be defective and how you will manage and contain the incident.

- Thinking back to the communication plan I discussed in *Chapter 4, 'Communication,'* include the upstream and downstream communication strategy to affected parties when you have cause to believe there may be a potential issue with your products or services, that requires action on behalf of the recipient. Remember that communications are both proactive and reactive. It is prudent to warn consumers or organizations about potential hazards or dangers so they can determine their own risk factors when making decisions.

- Document the level of support that you will provide to the interested parties that may be affected directly, or indirectly because of the identified issue or incident.

- Identify the process for escalation if an issue or incident cannot be contained.

Note: If the organization is calculating the type and scale of injuries that may or may not be acceptable, this is not a 'people-first' organization. I shall discuss more on why this is such an important element in *Chapter 17, People*

In the next chapter, I shall discuss the importance of demonstrating *'Empathy'* for those affected by a major incident, whether directly or indirectly.

CHAPTER 6
Empathy

E = EMPATHY

"Nobody cares how much you know until they know how much you care."

—Theodore Roosevelt, Former U.S. President

Having empathy and compassion for others is a deep and emotive subject that has been brought to the forefront by the COVID 19 global pandemic.

Empathy is a deeper appreciation and understanding of how each interaction you have impacts those most affected, whether directly or indirectly. Your words and actions have a lasting effect, whether you realize it or not.

Structure

In this chapter, I will be discussing the following:

- Perils of victim blaming
- Demonstrating empathy for people
- Demonstrating empathy for organizations

Objectives

A key objective of this chapter is to explore why empathy is so much more than just saying and doing the right thing. It is about having self-awareness and appreciation for how an individual or organization may be coping with a major incident and crisis and how your actions can determine whether people will respond positively or negatively to the situation.

Perils of victim blaming

Every day we hear stories of cyberattacks where millions of records or sensitive data have been breached—the countless people and companies who have fallen foul of theft, fraud, extortion, and espionage.

Yet we treat them with contempt and blame them for not defending themselves better, despite being victims of a crime. Whether the victim is an individual or an organization, if they feel that they will be mistreated, or with contempt for '*allowing*' an attack to happen, or for not doing more to prevent the impact, they may be less likely to be open and truthful about the circumstances of the incident.

This causes two issues –

- Individuals or organizations are less likely to admit that they have been a victim of an incident or attack, and
- They are more likely to downplay it, even dismissing the gravity of the situation.

The impact of both issues means that the true extent of incidents, and our ability to learn from them, are significantly impacted. In addition, this creates further issues with the requirements for being *'Believable.'*

We forget that these are real people who have been impacted, and these incidents can cause a devastating financial, social, and emotional impact.

Demonstrating empathy for people

Empathy means understanding what is happening from the people's perspective, and is it within your capacity to offer support, guidance, or help?

Being empathetic is not an easy trait. Simply stating you have empathy for someone's situation is not enough. Being a compassionate leader requires self-awareness and consciously acting in the right way for the right reasons. *'Empathy'* and *'Gravitas'* are intrinsically linked, can be powerful, and are potent attributes to demonstrate leadership in times of crisis.

Empathy for another person and their situation is not just a good thing for the employees in your organization, but it is also essential for the business. Being able to pre-empt and manage the stressors that people may be facing as part of their day-to-day working life and acknowledging when there is a change in the environment or social dynamics of the workplace can help to address and alleviate insider risks.

Often, this can be as simple as people being able to acknowledge where they have made a mistake or need extra support. Still, in some cases, it can also reduce the propensity for that person to demonstrate malicious intent, particularly if they feel that they are being ignored or that the organization is increasing rather than decreasing the stress factors.

This can reach a breaking point when people are in the middle of a major incident, particularly one that extends into weeks and months, or even several years, in the case of the global pandemic.

A key output of the pandemic is how people have become accustomed to stating that this is 'the new normal.' This term is often used to describe something previously unfamiliar or unusual but is now accepted as common or normal.

Firstly, this is an over-generalist statement, as each person's perception of normality differs, and there can be variances based on culture and people's experience of being in these situations. It also disregards the emotional distress and grief many people may have experienced during this period. Therefore, it is important not to downplay how people may feel and cope in the short, medium, and long term and what adjustments, if any, may be needed.

Simply expressing that this experience is typical or expected can also increase the stress that people may be under. If this is dismissed, it can create an environment that breeds contempt.

Being empathetic means considering each person as an individual and is intricately linked to that person's emotional resilience. This does not mean that an individual's manager needs to be personally accountable for that person's emotional state, but it does mean that the organization needs to have a range of mechanisms and support in place that enables the individual to have access to *'Wellbeing'* resources, that they can take advantage of, and where they feel fully supported.

As identified previously, culture is a crucial factor in crisis response. A strong culture that puts people at the heart of the organization will achieve the best results from those people when they feel safe and secure, and their needs are being met. We discuss this further in *Chapter 17, People.*

Demonstrating empathy for organizations

Empathy requires both an inward and outward focus. So, as much as we need to consider how we demonstrate empathy to people inside our organization, we also need to consider how we show empathy to people working across other organizations who may have also experienced a major incident or crisis and how we respond to this.

Consider the situation they find themselves in, especially if they are prevented or delayed in delivering their products and services. Is your automatic action to seek recourse through service penalties or other contractual means, or is it within your power or gift to assist?

An excellent example of where many organizations have rallied to assist is again due to the COVID19 pandemic. Either to divert or to procure additional services for those on the front line, providing emergency care or humanitarian aid. People and organizations generally became more tolerant and expectant of delays and adjusted their plans accordingly.

This mustn't lead to complacency, as there is still an expectation that the organization is working to resolve the situation and to bring services back into agreed tolerances. The goodwill and grace that was provided can quickly diminish.

What you expect from others is a good indicator of what others should expect of you in return. With organizations becoming increasingly interconnected and dependent on each other, a strategy that centers on mutual benefit and aid during times of crisis will deliver the most resilience. We shall explore the intricacies of the supply chain further, in *Chapter 22, Underdog.*

Conclusion

In this chapter, we have explored why empathy is important to demonstrate during a major incident or crisis and why we need to be mindful of who may be most impacted by the incident, either directly or indirectly. As we shall continue to discuss in subsequent chapters, empathy and self-awareness are crucial to ensuring that people remain front and center in our decisions.

Reflection

- Think back to previous incidents within your organization and how they were handled. Did the organization demonstrate empathy?

- Do you have mechanisms in place to help gauge where people have become despondent with the organization's messaging?

Suggested actions

- Provide organizational leaders and managers with training and guidance on empathy and sincerity.

- Provide managers and leaders with the mechanisms and support for establishing how people feel in the organization and how this can escalate.

In the next chapter, I shall discuss the importance of establishing *'Facts'*. This is a crucial area for determining the basis of key decisions that need to be made at the outset of a major incident, as we explored in *Chapter 2, Actions*. As discussed in the previous chapter, it is also a determining in performing appropriate *'Diligence.'*

CHAPTER 7
Facts

F = FACTS

"Facts do not cease to exist because they are ignored."

—*Aldous Huxley, English Writer, and Philosopher*

During any major incident, we must separate the facts from fiction.

Facts are those things we know to be true, backed up with credible evidence. Fiction is what we make up to fill the gaps in our knowledge.

Things that can typically be regarded as fiction:

- Lies

- Rumors

- Deception

- Defamation

- Disinformation

- Speculation

- Propaganda

- Non-credible sources

The problem is that it gets harder to tell the difference over time because the fiction is interwoven with the facts.

So, the information we base our decisions on and subsequent actions are flawed, which can have profound consequences.

Structure

In this chapter, I will discuss the following-

- The pursuit of truth

- Misinformation versus disinformation

- Emerging impact of disinformation campaigns

- Fact-checking

- Digital forensics

Objectives

This chapter explains why we must separate facts from fiction in the pursuit of truth. As discussed in *Chapter 2, Action*, our ability to make informed decisions, is predicated on establishing the accuracy and source of information we rely upon.

I shall explore the dangers of misinformation and disinformation and why we need to fact-check information being utilized and shared within and outside the organization. We shall also consider the importance of utilizing digital forensics to establish a detailed timeline to verify what happened and when.

The pursuit of truth

As identified through previous chapters in our pursuit of the truth, we need to consider the culture we have enabled - is it one where people can be honest about their mistakes, or do they cover them up out of fear of retribution and blame?

Misinformation versus disinformation

An issue that can often occur when establishing facts is verifying the source and accuracy of the information you may rely upon. This is particularly relevant when relying on digital media, which may have been copied or altered over time, especially if it has been downloaded or uploaded from social media multiple times.

This is particularly relevant in the case of synthetic media, which has been purposely created to manipulate certain sectors of the population or their belief systems.

Let us look at some definitions of misinformation, disinformation, fake news, and deep fakes so that we can understand why these can be harmful to individuals and organizations during a crisis:

- **Misinformation** is the most common example and is typically the spread of false or incorrect information, regardless of whether there is an intent to mislead or deceive the audience.

- **Disinformation** is designed to mislead, manipulate, or sway the audience's opinion by promoting biased and prejudiced information, such as propaganda.

- **Fake news** is purposefully crafted, emotionally charged, misleading or fabricated information that mimics the form of mainstream news. It is often sensationalist and large-scale to grab the audience's attention.

- **Deepfakes** are a new and particularly challenging type of audio, video, or image disinformation used maliciously. The technology used to mimic or change voice patterns synthetically is often referred to as voice skin. It typically utilizes artificial intelligence to replace or alter the speech or image of a person in the original media content with someone else in a way that makes it look or sound authentic.

Emerging impact of disinformation campaigns

The rise and use of disinformation for the mass manipulation of people has been growing over the last few years. Unlike some campaigns that can be used to target individuals or organizations, disinformation campaigns aim to target entire communities and even countries. The impact of disinformation could almost be a chapter in its own right, as it is an important factor for determining how information is obtained and utilized by the organization and how they utilize this to make strategic and tactical decisions.

The use of disinformation is often politically motivated, and with widespread data sources and content, this has generated an *'information war,'* which can cause large-scale social and economic unrest. This is a particular tactic that nation-state actors have demonstrated. We shall explore this further when analyzing some of the tactics used in a *'hybrid war'* in *Chapter 12, 'Knowledge'*.

In addition, the deliberate targeting of sub-groups of susceptible people can lead to radicalization, where they start to support extreme ideologies, which can potentially draw them into acts of terrorism. This is a form of psychological manipulation.

While perhaps not as extreme, activists also use disinformation to target subgroups of people to disrupt organizations through protest or sabotage. Organizations can find themselves targets through association due to the countries, companies, or individuals they trade with.

Hactivism is a form of activism that attempts to gain remote access to the organization's technology and operational infrastructure, to further their social or political cause. This can include the sabotage of systems and the exfiltration or destruction of sensitive data. They may also attempt to establish persistence within the network through collusion with employees. This needs to be considered as part of a broader insider risk strategy that assesses the privileges and sensitive information that groups of employees may have access to and how this could be abused, irrespective of the intent. I will circle back around to this towards the end of the book, where I discuss the necessity and importance of having a *'Zero Trust'* mindset.

Of worrying note is the increase in disinformation campaigns being utilized by one rival organization to another. Whilst corporate and industrial espionage is nothing new, the willingness to deliberately sabotage a competitor in a chosen market through the dissemination of false and libelous information is a key threat that organizations should be mindful of from a crisis response perspective. This may be done in a way that does not necessarily track back to the offending organization by way of fake product and service reviewers or complaints. Whilst attribution may be difficult to prove, corporate-fueled disinformation campaigns and the impact this can have during pivotal times – such as product launches, mergers, and acquisitions should be actively monitored.

Here are some key questions that organizations should consider when assessing the potential impact of a disinformation campaign.

- **What is the overall narrative?** What is the impact of what is being portrayed, and how could this be perceived by various stakeholders and interested parties?

- **What is your motivation for obtaining or sharing this information?** What is your role as a consumer of information, either from a personal or organizational perspective, and are you helping or hindering the situation?

- **Are you looking for an unbiased opinion, or are you looking to fuel and reinforce your own narrative?** What will you do with this information? Could someone be trying to manipulate the outcome of a decision because of providing this information?

- **What is the motivation behind the source of information?** What do they get out of sharing incorrect or false information? Is there a political agenda, or do they receive some form of financial gain from sharing *'clickbait' style* news?

- **What is the role of influencers, and how are they compensated or rewarded?** Influencers typically have amassed a large following on social media and can be used in advertising to build trust or distrust in brands and ideologies. The more followers that are amassed, the more lucrative this can be, as this can drive higher audiences and revenues, particularly if the influencer site includes advertising and compensation based on likes and shares.

Consider whether their opinion is widely respected and what is their background and qualification. Are they being paid to have their own opinion about a product or service, or is it just the organization's opinion? Could this organization or person be trying to promote their own product, service, or viewpoint to the detriment of others?

When a person chooses to follow or engage with an influencer, it can be because they have an affinity with the person or the subject they are promoting. They are more likely to relate them to positive emotions, so their critical thinking and challenge of the content may not be engaged.

Be mindful that people can be paid to spread a message, even if they do not believe it or understand it. Similarly, influencers may also be duped into believing they are supporting a worthy cause and may also be subjected to manipulation.

An example of how influencers can be utilized to reinforce and promote a specific narrative is in relation to the COVID 19 vaccines. In research[1] conducted by the *Center for Countering Digital Hate (CCDH)*, it is claimed that prominent *'anti-vaxxers'* view COVID as a historic opportunity for them to reach larger numbers of the public and to create long-lasting distrust in the effectiveness, safety, and necessity for vaccination. They have developed a sophisticated playbook for spreading uncertainty, converting *'vaccine-hesitant'* people into committed anti-vaxxers through online subcultures that reside on social media channels

Not only do such campaigns have an impact on those people being actively targeted, but they can also have a detrimental impact on pharmaceutical organizations, researchers, and medical professionals. This can lead people within the organizations to feel anxious or distressed if they do become victims of activism.

We shall further highlight how nation-state threat actors can utilize emotive subjects to further enhance their own rhetoric in the case study on the Russian invasion of Ukraine and the *'hybrid war'* in *Chapter 12, Knowledge.*

The answers to some of these questions should consider the ethical and social dilemmas because of inadvertently sharing or believing disinformation campaigns. Similarly, whilst misinformation does not have malicious intent, it can still cause harm to individuals or organizations and have a high impact.

Simply stating you were not aware that the information you relied upon is wrong or misleading is not going to be a reliable defense and calls into subsequent issues with *'Justice'*.

There is an expectation that you have performed a degree of *'Diligence'* before considering how you will utilize or share the information and the consequences if the data is later found to be inaccurate or false.

Fact checking

Due to the propensity and growth of disinformation, there are several resources and strategies that organizations can deploy to determine the source and accuracy of information. This can include:

- Stay informed and have awareness about the emerging trends for misinformation and disinformation. Promote media literacy for those that need to be aware of the risks and that actively need to utilize the information. This can be especially relevant for those people working in marketing or product development.

---

1 Center for Countering Digital Hate, The Anti-Vax Playbook, 23rd December 2022, https://counterhate.com/wp-content/uploads/2022/05/210106-The-Anti-Vaxx-Playbook.pdf (retrieved 16th August 2022)

- Stop and think before you reshare information and take a moment to engage your critical thinking skills. Allow the fast-acting emotional response to pass, particularly when dealing with sensationalist or emotive materials. The way in which stories are written, or the images portrayed, may be designed to elicit a strong emotional response and may be deliberately targeted. This is often referred to as *'yellow journalism,* where a sensationalist headline or image is utilized to grab the reader's attention rather than factual content.

- Consider the *'Action'* that you expect people to take or not take because of the information and potential consequences of sharing or not sharing this information.

- Take the time to find a secondary reference to the content you are reliant on. Use at least one trusted news provider and determine if that information is confirmed or disputed by other independent sources.

- When citing the source of information, be careful not to just cite what the source was but when it was accessed. This means that should the author alter the content of the article or post on social media, you can verify when it was accessed or utilized prior to the change. A good example of this also includes posts that generate multiple likes, to then have the content of the post changed but still have the same likes, to make people assume that a large number of people agree or support the narrative.

- Utilize advanced searches where available. Many internet search engines have a reverse image search facility to verify the source of a photograph or screenshot. Look for visually similar images and verify when and where they were published and by whom. Have the words and pictures been altered, or is it out of context? If the same images have been utilized in different scenarios, this can be indicative that the image has been misused as a ploy to deliberately deceive the recipient.

- Utilize fact-checking sites to verify whether the story or content has already been refuted. Some of the larger media outlets, such as the BBC or Reuters, invest considerable effort in verification and provide all their sources so that you can validate their research for yourself.

Digital forensics

Dependent on the nature and scale of the incident, it may be necessary to utilize digital forensics to provide a sequence and catalog of events, to substantiate and support any subsequent investigation, and to verify the information that has been collated.

In the event of a criminal or regulatory investigation, there may be a need to provide evidence and a chain of custody in terms of who did what and when and to prove that the systems and records have not been tampered with. In the event of a criminal or legislative investigation, this may include the seizure of property, which should be considered as a risk to availability, security, or privacy. The removal of such property may also hinder recovery efforts.

In many ways, the requirements for verifying sources, and verifying the accuracy of the information, follow a similar path to that discussed with disinformation and fact checking. The main difference is that this information and evidence trail has typically derived from within the organization's own technology systems and networks.

For any 'Investigation,' there is a need to assume that the output may be relied upon for legal or regulatory purposes and needs to be treated in the same way as evidence utilized in criminal or civil prosecution.

Some key considerations for digital forensics:

- Utilize specialist and certified practitioners with proven credibility and knowledge of the underpinning technologies and systems.

- Follow documented codes of practice applicable to the jurisdiction, which may require different controls to be evidenced.

- Maintain the highest ethical standards and respect the confidentiality and privacy of organizations and individuals. This may require the pseudonymization of data to prevent unconscious bias.

- Ensure there are no preconceived ideas on what you are expecting to find or not find, and do not be swayed to limit the scope of the review.

- There should be no presumption of guilt based on what has been reported in the media or through other sources.

- Identify and catalog the location and source of data before touching it. This can include recording timestamps and embedded metadata.

- Perform appropriate due diligence to preserve all materials for verification by interested parties.

- Report exactly what has been found or not found without speculation or ambiguity.

- Consider how the information will be utilized by the recipient and the potential consequences if misused or if the results are later established to be inaccurate or misleading.

- Determine whether independent verification and cross-checking of evidence are required prior to publication.

Conclusion

In this chapter, we explored the importance of fact-checking the source and accuracy of the information that we may be reliant on during a major incident or crisis. We discussed the difference between misinformation and disinformation and how such campaigns are being utilized to manipulate or radicalize groups of people. It made us consider the will and motivation behind individuals or organizations that attempt to build trust or mistrust in specific ideologies and why promoting digital literacy is a must for every organization.

Reflection

- Does your organization have a strategy and plan for managing and counteracting misinformation and disinformation?

- Consider the type of information that the organization may produce to validate marketing or other claims in relation to your products and services and how people may make decisions based on those claims

- Consider if your organization may be a specific target for activism and how to counteract this.

- Are you utilizing influencers to promote different aspects of your brand, including products and services? Are they free to make their own decision, or are they being paid to make specific endorsements? Consider the reliance that consumers may have on that person and their level of credibility. Does this engender trust, or can it be called into dispute?

Suggested actions

- Thinking back to the action plan, in *Chapter 2, 'Action'* where I spoke about the decision trees and information that may be required to enable effective decision-making. Consider the type and relevancy of trusted sources and the potential danger of relying on comments or stories made on social media.

- Does the overall incident response and crisis strategy identify a list of specialist organizations that can be called upon at short notice to provide additional services? Has the organization's credibility and capability been validated, and can they be relied upon? This may also include the addition of temporary staff who have been called to help with the incident.

- Ensure that what you are portraying as facts, through communications with interested parties, has been validated as such. Or where further information or independent verification is needed.

- Create a process for identifying and escalating defamatory and incorrect statements about your products and statements and the process by which this is handled.

In the next chapter, I shall explore the importance of 'Gravitas'. This links back to the previous chapter on 'Empathy,' where both traits combined are important for demonstrating trust and establishing a rapport with interested parties.

CHAPTER 8
Gravitas

Think back to a time in your life when you came across someone who you thought was a natural leader. Someone who you wanted to follow, not because you had to, but because you wanted to.

You just knew you could trust in their ability, and they would guide you and have your best interests at heart.

Not only did these person(s) have knowledge and experience, but they also demonstrated a few other traits, such as courage, compassion, respect, empathy, humility, and honesty.

They demonstrated all these things, not just in their words but in their judgment, the decisions they made, and the actions that followed.

This person(s) has gravitas.

Structure

In this chapter, I will discuss the following-

- Leadership and gravitas
- Demonstrating gravitas

Objectives

This chapter aims to highlight why gravitas is an essential trait for building trust during a major incident or crisis. As we shall explore, the most senior person in the organization is not always the one that holds the most gravitas. Therefore when selecting the most appropriate leaders to manage different aspects of the incident response, gravitas is a key consideration.

Leadership and gravitas

Gravitas is more than just having good leadership skills. It is the trust and belief that people have in this person(s) that really stands out. They are typically charismatic leaders whom others will be drawn to.

It is this person(s) that you want to lead and guide people through a crisis.

This is plural because there will be people with different skill sets and experiences that you may need at various times.

And remember, the person(s) who yields the most power are not always the ones with the most gravitas.

In crises, there is a tendency to utilize the most senior person in the company to make public statements. However, as we identified in *Chapter 4, Communication*, and the case study on the handling of communications in the case of the Deep-Water Horizon oil spill, this person does not necessarily have gravitas.

Of course, people can receive training on developing core skills, but gravitas is a trait remarkably like trust in that it tends to be something that has developed over a period, and one requires a degree of humility and dignity when faced with difficult situations. There is perhaps a vulnerability there that allows people to see the human side of the organization. This should not be seen as a sign of weakness in the individual or organization but as a way of establishing trust, and it can be a powerful trait when displayed in the right way.

Gravitas, therefore, is a quality rather than a specific skill, and much like '*Empathy,*' it comes with a willingness and desire to seek '*Justice.*' There is often an overwhelming desire for this person(s) to demonstrate integrity.

As we highlighted, and for a good reason, a person with gravitas can be a powerful leader and is someone that people naturally want to follow, as opposed to someone that they need to follow because of seniority.

Demonstrating gravitas

Some common traits of people that have gravitas, which are key strengths in a crisis, include:

- The ability to influence the people around them
- Utilize words and actions that deliver impact
- Hold a captive audience irrespective of size
- Remain calm under pressure
- Consider their actions and how people may perceive them and adjust accordingly

Suppose the most senior person(s) is also the one that carries gravitas. In that case, the organization will be extremely fortunate to have this person(s) at the helm, as the organization is potentially already demonstrating the virtues of what it takes to lead the organization through a crisis, and beyond.

This may or may not be the same person(s) in your organization. Still, either way, it is important to identify the person(s) that has the gravitas to win hearts and minds, as well as the ability to follow through on stated objectives and actions, no matter how difficult these may be. It is OK to acknowledge that crisis leaders may be differentiated from other leaders in the organization.

Conclusion

In this chapter, we explored the importance of demonstrating gravitas and how this is also intrinsically linked to empathy. It is about one of the key elements that differentiate leaders in a crisis, and people will remember how you made them feel more than what you said.

Reflection

- Consider the people and personalities involved in the incident and crisis management process, are the leaders and spokespeople based on hierarchy or gravitas?

- Are there different people that may be better for communication or establishing rapport with different stakeholders

Suggested actions

- Thinking back to the action plan in *Chapter 2, Action*, and the communication strategy in *Chapter 4, 'Communication'*, where I asked you to document the owners of the actions, and decision-makers, consider which of these people have the right gravitas to lead in difficult situations. Are some of the people better suited to internal or external facing roles?

- Determine the soft skills and training that people may require to demonstrate gravitas, particularly when faced with difficult situations or duress.

- Ensure that the leaders also receive emotional support and guidance in the same way as other employees, as they are potentially expected to create a lot of weight and responsibility on their soldiers.

As identified in *Chapter 3, Believable* this is intricately linked to *'Honesty'* which is what we will explore in the next chapter. It is another important factor in demonstrating integrity and trust.

CHAPTER 9
Honesty

As children, we are taught that honesty is the best policy. But do we really hold this virtue in high regard?

Have we fostered the right culture and environment that enables people to step forward and admit their mistakes or to feel empowered to highlight wrongdoing or grievance?

Sometimes, we are told it is OK to tell a trivial lie if we are protecting that person or do not want to hurt their feelings. Something we must ask ourselves, and that we should reflect on, is who are we really protecting in that scenario? Chances are it is us that want to avoid the subject or confrontation, so we convince ourselves we are doing it for the greater good.

There have been times in my career when I was put in difficult situations where being honest and reporting on what I found through incidents, exercises or audits was discouraged because of the negative connotations, or there was concern about how management would react to seeing lots of '*red*' in a report.

This made me feel very uneasy because if it can happen once, it can happen many times. The misreporting and downplaying of incidents and audits can lead to more severe events if left unsolved, as we shall explore in some of the case studies and anecdotes.

Structure

In this chapter, I will discuss the following-

- Demonstrating integrity
- Believability versus honesty
- Dealing with whistleblowing
- Dealing with grievances

Objectives

This chapter aims to highlight why honesty is still the best policy and why there is a difference between believability and honesty when it comes to demonstrating integrity and trust. I shall explore what happens when there is mistrust from within the organization and how this can lead to grievances and whistleblowing. Your *Actions* often speak louder than words, and therefore what you choose to do next is just as important as what you say.

Demonstrating integrity

Having integrity is important, as is recording where someone has asked you to alter or remove something against your recommendation or judgment. This is not about having an '*I told you so*' moment down the road but being able to verify why this was not reported or actioned at the time. It could be that the person did not appreciate or understand why this was a critical issue or that there was information missing that would have led to a different conclusion. This is one of the reasons why I talked about accumulating and aggregating information on reported issues and risks from across the organization to provide a '*big-picture* view of the situation.

Believability versus honesty

Now, you may be thinking *Believability* and *Honesty* are the same things. I would like to hope that these are strong virtues that would be utilized together in a crisis but being believable does not necessarily mean that you are being honest!

You can come across as being believable whilst being deliberately deceptive, as you are trying to convince people that you are trustworthy when in fact, you are not. This also brings into issues of integrity.

Of course, this could be a deliberate ploy by the organization to put out misleading information. Still, you need to weigh up the consequences of these actions, and the damage that can occur to the organization, is what can only be described as a short-term (and narrow-sighted) gain at best.

Cast your mind back to the opening *Introduction*, where I talked about the power of hindsight and foresight. Things have a nasty habit of resurfacing when you least expect it, and history has a habit of repeating itself. We will explore more about the value of hindsight in *Chapter 10, Investigation*.

This is further amplified in a digital environment, where nothing is ever truly deleted or forgotten. In fact, in a major incident, the public and the media have long memories and will potentially look for past examples to collaborate on the legitimacy of the story or, conversely, look for instances where it is contradictory.

Hopefully, I have established by now that this book is about sharing best practices and principles. Hence, I do not condone being deliberately deceptive. There may be instances where information that was relied upon is later found to be inaccurate, and hence it is important to correct and verify this information as quickly as possible once known.

Dealing with whistleblowing

Typically, this involves the reporting of an event or series of events of such magnitude that it requires legal protection or anonymity so that the person(s) do not fear retribution, dismissal, or further legal action.

The mere fact that a whistleblowing policy is required says a lot about the culture within the organization. Part of the policies of the organization should encourage employees to come forward and voice any concerns they have to help cultivate a culture of transparency in the workplace.

Arguably if the organization already has a culture of openness and transparency and enables people to come forward, and voice their concerns to management, then a whistleblowing policy would not be needed but is still required for many organizations.

Dealing with grievances

People may prefer to stay quiet and say nothing at all if they think they will be ignored or no action will be taken.

Conversely, people may put action into their own hands by bypassing organizational policies and processes and leaking sensitive information to external parties, which may include the media or activists. The employee(s) with the grievance often want or need to feel their concerns are validated and may leak information in the hope that it will lead to positive action or change but may also do this for malicious or nefarious reasons.

The exfiltration and leaking of sensitive information, irrespective of the underpinning rationale, needs to be treated as a crisis when considered against the will and motivation of the person(s) that has the grievance, the type of information exposed, and the subsequent impact on the organization. This could also lead to issues with litigation.

If the person(s) feel that they have nothing to lose at this point, it may also trigger subsequent actions regarding the deliberate sabotage of critical infrastructure or business processes, and hence whistleblowing and grievances should also be considered as part of an insider risk strategy and program.

There is a need to consider how you will support and encourage more people to come out of the shadows, bring issues to your attention before they turn into major incidents, and help the organization ultimately do better. A core aspect of this comes down to *'Empathy'*, where we need to develop a deep understanding and appreciation of why certain situations may trigger stressors and be emotive for certain employees.

One of the main objectives of this book is to prevent an incident or breach from happening in the first place by moving from a proactive to a reactive state. This may sound contradictory when considered against an assume compromise or failure mindset, but the objective is to reduce the probability and / or impact of an incident should it occur by taking preemptive steps that can limit exposure or damage.

Let us think about how we really can make honesty the best policy for our people.

Conclusion

In this chapter, I discussed the importance of honesty and integrity in building trust. I also explored the dangers where there is mistrust and why people will be more likely to take their grievances into their own hands if they don't believe in what you say or the actions you take. There is a need to consider the harm that whistleblowing and leakage of sensitive information may have on the organization. So it needs to be considered as part of the overall crisis response.

Reflection

- Consider your organization's overall culture and whether there are mechanisms in place for people to actively report mistakes or grievances. Is this done in a way that supports those who have been honest, or is there a fear of negative action?

- Consider whether there may be previous or current events where the organization may have mishandled the incident and whether there are opportunities to rectify this.

- Consider the current process for handling grievances or whistleblowing and what may have already been reported. Is there a pattern emerging in terms of what is being reported and why?

- What is the organization's attitude towards people who have raised a grievance? Are they treated with respect or contempt?

- Are there mechanisms to protect unauthorized access, exfiltration of sensitive information, or sabotage critical infrastructure?

Suggested actions

- Thinking back to *Chapter 7, Facts*, provide a commitment to be open, transparent, and honest about the facts as they arise, even those that may portray the organization in a negative light. For example, missed or ignored warning signs?

- Ensure that people know how to report a grievance or other issues and how they can expect to be acknowledged and treated. Can people make anonymous reports, and how is privacy protected?

- Instigate a process for analyzing and detecting anomalies in behavior as part of an insider threat program. This should cater to identifying malicious as well as non-malicious activity and be designed in a way that protects against unconscious bias and maintains privacy by applying pseudonyms to data and assets.

- Instigate a data classification and information protection program, to identify and prevent the mass exfiltration of sensitive data, in the case of whistleblowing, or other scenarios.

In the next chapter, I shall explore the importance of performing a thorough 'Investigation' in the pursuit of the truth. As we have identified, this needs to start from a position of being open, honest, and transparent, to engender trust in the organization.

CHAPTER 10
Investigation

I = INVESTIGATION

"Wisdom is not acquired save as the result of an investigation."

—*Sara Teasdale, U.S. Poet*

If we accept that you should have an assume failure and compromise mindset and that an incident could happen at any time, then you need mechanisms that enable you to detect and respond as efficiently and effectively as possible.

Structure

In this chapter, I will discuss the following:

- Co-ordinating the investigation

- Learning from public inquiries

- Case study 2: Grenfell Tower Block fire

- Results of investigations

Objectives

As soon as an incident has been declared resolved, it will be necessary to investigate what happened and why. The aim of this chapter is to determine how the investigation should be coordinated and how the results will be shared. There is much that can be learned from public inquiries, and so we shall explore the second case study, where we consider some of the common factors that are reported from multiple inquiries.

Co-ordinating the investigation

Often the first time we become aware of a major incident is when the proverbial hits the fan.

But this is NOT the start of the incident.

The events that led up to the failure or compromise happened way before this. The subsequent investigation, therefore, requires us to roll the clock backward to critically review what happened. In *Chapter 12, Lessons*, I shall explore how hindsight is a valuable tool for enabling foresight and why this is often overlooked.

You will need to be able to correlate potentially disparate sources of information to determine the key '*Facts*' and sequence of events that caused the incident to manifest in the way that it did. This can also be exasperated by external factors, so it is important that the investigation looks beyond internal information and this is collaborated with external sources and interested parties, where applicable. This should include information and feedback derived from customers, partners, and media as examples.

'*Questions*' to ask ourselves relate to the availability, quality, and accuracy of actions, audit logs, change records, system updates, test results, and so on. We require a healthy degree of skepticism rather than cynicism when determining the legitimacy and sources of information that we are reliant on. Therefore it is encouraged that you should question some of the information provided rather than just accepting it at face value. We explore this area further in *Chapter 18, Questions*, when we consider the key questions to ask ourselves in advance of an incident, as well as post-incident.

We need to consider how far back in time we can realistically go and do we have the right investigative and forensic capabilities to do that or do we have gaps in our process and knowledge? You will need to verify whether the information is available and to what extent, and whether that information has been altered or deleted in any way, which is a key aspect of *'Diligence'*. If these questions cannot easily be verified, then chances are that you already have gaps in *'Knowledge'* which is going to hinder the investigation.

Without this insight, it is highly probable that there will be repeated incidents, or failures, because you are unable to verify or articulate the extent of the failure and whether this is still a substantial risk. This may also increase the overall liability, and raises questions on the potential for negligence, as we identify in the next chapter on *'Justice.'* There needs to be a willingness and desire to want to get to the truth, no matter how hard that may be.

It is, therefore, important not to wait until you have an incident to find you have a gap.

Learning from public inquiries

Reports from public inquiries are a good example of where systematic failings by the organization can lead to an incident of such magnitude that it has resulted in the loss of life, which often could have been avoided through increased diligence. Whilst such events are rare, the results of the inquiries are made public as a means of identifying opportunities for improvement and holding those responsible to account.

Dependent on the gravity and seriousness of the incident, which gave rise to the public inquiry, these can often be exceptionally long and detailed, with multiple sub-sections, witness statements, and forensic reports. When trying to establish a core set of lessons and key findings that can be acted upon, referring to the executive summary of the report can yield a lot of information and opportunities for improvement, which are summarized in an easy-to-digest way.

The first major incident and public inquiry I took an interest in was the Piper Alpha oil rig disaster[1], which occurred on the north coast of Scotland on 6 July 1988. The explosion and resulting fires killed 167 people, including two crew members of a rescue vessel.

---

1 BBC Archives, Piper Alpha Oil Rig Disaster, (7 July 1988) https://www.bbc.co.uk/archive/piper-al-pha-oil-rig-disaster-1988/zkdwr2p, retrieved 21 July 2022

I was only 12 years old, but there were multiple news stories and documentaries made as a result over a period of several years. The resulting public inquiry[2] would be the first time I would learn about how systematic failings across disparate areas can accumulate, over time, into a major disaster. Multiple warnings and opportunities to fix underpinning issues were often ignored until catastrophe struck.

Over the course of my career in business continuity, crisis management, and cybersecurity, I have taken an avid interest in reading post-incident reviews and public inquiry reports.

One thing that struck me was how similar many of the findings were and how we have a poor habit of learning 'Lessons'.

Case study 2

The next case study is an example of a more recent public inquiry to illustrate some of the common findings and failings that can occur across many incidents:

Case Study 2
Grenfell Tower Block Fire
The United Kingdom, 2017
Summary of incident
Grenfell Tower was a 24-story block of apartments in North Kensington, London.
On 24th June 2017, a fire broke out in the kitchen of one of the apartments on the 4th floor, which rapidly engulfed the building, leading to seventy-two deaths.
It was the deadliest structural fire in the UK since the 1988 Piper Alpha oil rig disaster and the worst UK residential fire since World War II.
Apartments in UK multi-story blocks are typically designed to withstand a fire long enough to enable the emergency services to reach the building and put out the fire before impacting neighboring apartments. In such circumstances, residents are informed not to leave their apartments but to stay where they are until help arrives.
However, between 2015-16 the Grenfell Tower underwent a major renovation, which included new cladding to improve the heating and efficiency of the building and general external appearance. The resulting gap between the cladding and the exterior of the building contributed to the fire spreading rapidly out of control, trapping people inside.

2 Health & Safety Executive, The Public Enquiry into the Piper Alpha Disaster, Volumes 1 and 2, (November 1990), https://www.hse.gov.uk/offshore/piper-alpha-disaster-public-inquiry.htm (retrieved 21 July 2022)

The resulting public inquiry is being conducted in two phases[3]

- Phase 1 focused on the factual narrative of the events and was published on 30 October 2019.

- Phase 2 examines how Grenfell Tower came to be in a condition that allowed the fire to spread in the way identified by Phase 1.

(At the time of this book publication, Phase 2 has yet to be concluded. As of March 2022, the cost of the inquiry alone is £142 million. Updates on the public inquiry are available at the link shown in the footnote)

Analysis of the incident

For the purposes of this case study, the analysis is centered on the core findings of the '*Phase 1 Report Executive Summary*[4]', which addresses '*how*' the incident occurred. The conditions that gave way to '*why*' this happened are subject to Phase 2 of the inquiry, which is a core factor of establishing the true root cause, which I will explore further in *Chapters 25, X Marks the Spot*, and *Chapter 26, Why*.

- The principal reason the flames spread so rapidly was the presence of the new cladding, which acted as a source of fuel for the fire.

- Evidence suggested that the external walls of the building failed to comply with building regulations, as they did not resist the spread of fire, having regard to the height, use, and position of the building.

- Experienced incident commanders and senior officers attending the fire had not received training in the dangers associated with combustible cladding, even though they were aware that such fires could occur.

- National guidance at the time required fire and rescue services to draw up contingency evacuation plans for dealing with fires in high-rise buildings when the '*stay put*' strategy was untenable.

- There was no specific contingency plan for the evacuation of Grenfell Tower.

- The first incident commanders, although experienced, were juniors. They were faced with a situation for which they had not been properly prepared.

- The Police, Fire, and Ambulance services all declared major incidents at various times but had not communicated this with each other, which compounded the ability to effectively deal with an emergency of such magnitude

---

3. The Grenfell Tower Inquiry, set up 15 August 2017: https://www.grenfelltowerinquiry.org.uk/

4. Grenfell Tower Inquiry: Phase 1 Overview Report (October 2019), https://www.grenfelltowerinquiry.org.uk/phase-1-report (retrieved 23 July 2022)

- The Fire Brigade continued to rely on the *'stay put'* strategy, despite early indications that the building had suffered a total failure of compartmentation between apartments.

- No information about the number and source of emergency calls from residents was communicated to the incident commanders. Similarly, information about the spread of the fire and the results of rescue operations was not effectively shared with incident commanders, as pictures from the police helicopters and television news crews on the ground were not available to them.

- The control room staff faced an unprecedented number of emergency calls relating to the fire. Operators did not always obtain necessary information, such as apartment numbers, the number of people present, or whether people were disabled; nor did they always assess conditions at the callers' locations and hence the possibility of their escape.

- Control room operators had not been trained to handle simultaneous calls, on the implications of a decision to evacuate, or on the circumstances in which a caller should be advised to leave the building or stay put. They were not aware of the danger of assuming that crews would always reach callers. As a result, they gave assurances that were not well-founded.

- Channels of communication between the control room and the incident on the ground were often improvised and prone to error. Call operators did not know enough about conditions in the tower or the progress of responses to individual calls, so they lacked a sound basis for telling callers whether help was on its way.

- By the time the *'stay put'* order was changed to one of mass evacuation, the control room operators had not been made aware that this was an order and not a recommendation. In addition, by this point, many residents had found their exits blocked by fire, or smoke.

As well as the Phase 1 public inquiry report, a subsequent BBC 2 documentary televised in October 2018 would highlight *'The Fires that Foretold Grenfell*[5]', pointing to similar high-rise fires that had taken place across the UK in 1973, 1991, 1999, 2005 and 2009, each of which resulted in multiple fatalities. This led some journalists and investigators to state that the Grenfell fire was not just an accident but a *'social crime.'*

5. BBC News, 'Grenfell Tower: The Fires that foretold the tragedy': https://www.bbc.co.uk/news/uk-england-45982810

Lessons we can learn from this:

The following lessons are intended to be generic rather than specific to just the Grenfell Tower fire incident (which can be found in the Phase 1 Inquiry Report) and are provided to highlight many similarities and lessons learned that can be applied to multiple events and scenarios.

These can help serve to lessen the probability or impact of a major incident from occurring:

Changes in design and use

- Contingency plans often fail because changes have not been included in the plans or have not been effectively communicated:

- Consider how any changes or additions can affect the original design and use of the building, technology, or product and the impacts that this may have in terms of people's knowledge and understanding of the changes.

- The assessment and impact of the change should consider how it alters the integrity, safety, security, and reliability of the product or service, for the worse or better.

- Change control procedures need to determine what documentation, training, and exercises need to be performed to verify the effectiveness and implementation of the change.

- Consider the level of flexibility that people have and their resistance to accepting change. Those who have low levels of flexibility will be more stuck in their ways than those with higher levels of flexibility which are able to adjust their mindset and emotions to the changing environment.

- Consider that some people may not be in a position to change for reasons of accessibility or disability.

Communication

As stated in *Chapter 4, Communication*, effective communications are critical in a major incident. Some additional considerations relating to this case study and other public inquiries include the following:

- Importance of upstream and downstream communications to ensure this is not one way.

- Ensure that communication is not performed at a hierarchal level, but in unison. For example, avoiding the delay that can happen when people are expecting communication to go all the way to the top, and then back down again before action is communicated or taken.

- Verify that communications have been received, understood, and actioned as expected.

- Consider workarounds and alternative methods of communication if primary communication channels do not work, are overloaded, or shut off.

- Instigate a direct line to the command-and-control function. Do not rely on relaying messages when you have specific commands and instructions to provide to the operational and recovery teams on the ground.

- Communicate any changes in previous communications or directives. Ensure these are time and date-stamped and that these are updated to show if communications have been superseded.

- Instigate a process for handling large volumes of inbound and outbound calls from different stakeholders and the ability to scale and escalate. It is important that emergency calls are not ignored.

- Consider language and cultural barriers, with written and spoken language, and whether this needs to be translated or if interpreters may be required.

Command and control

- Establish and document the thresholds and guidance for determining and escalating a major incident.

- Consider the seniority and experience of key decision-makers and when and how they will be communicated with.

- Establish escalation and support for inexperienced or junior people, especially if they may be first on the scene and may not know what to do.

- People may be asked to step up to the next role if the primary role holders are unavailable. It is important that people understand other roles and responsibilities and whether there are expectations that they may be asked to perform those actions so that they feel confident to be able to perform those duties in an emergency.

- Consider the level of empowerment that people may have. Whilst we want to try and avoid the need for improvisation, there will be times when people will need to make decisions quickly to contain and manage the incident.

- Consider how people are deployed and the impact if those people are not performing those duties and actions. Consider whether people are multi-skilled to cover multiple areas or whether they are specialists and, therefore, cannot be redeployed.

- Consider what to do if there is a shortage of resources and reliance on third parties or contractors and their level of knowledge and experience. What additional support and supervision may be required until appropriate training has been provided, and how much authorization is required to enable them to fulfill their objectives?

Incident Response Plans

Often incident response plans can fail because they are so rigid with the instructions that they offer no guidance when things do not work as expected, causing panic and the need for improvisation. We shall discuss more incident response plans in *Chapter 20, Strategy*. Some further considerations include the following:

- Make a clear distinction between a recommendation and a specific order. People will need to understand the impact if expected actions are not performed. This is a crucial element of *Actions*.

Training and Awareness

Often incident response plans can fail because people have not received appropriate training. We shall discuss more on training and awareness in *Chapter 19, Resilience*. Some further considerations include the following:

- The training should acknowledge that things will not go to plan and how to handle difficult and challenging circumstances. This is part of the assume compromise and failure mindset.

- People will need to have a good understanding of the physical and digital environments that they will be required to work with and be trained in any changes or additions that alter the design or performance of the original design

- Perform short and regular refresher training on key principles so that this remains current and people are not overloaded with too much information.

Tests and exercises

This is an extension of training and awareness, where people can practice what they have learned in a safe and controlled environment. Some further considerations include the following:

- Perform a test and exercise after every major change.

- Exercises should be based on real-life incidents by taking input from previous incidents. This should also include '*Near-Misses.*'

- The aim of each exercise is to build confidence at each stage to the point where people can be fully immersed in an exercise that enables them to test each element of the plan in realistic conditions.

- This can often be an area where organizations are ill-prepared, as they have not considered or planned for a worst-case scenario.

Results of investigations

When performing your own investigation, there is a need to consider the depth and breadth of the findings, the interested parties involved, and their needs and expectations in terms of what is relevant to them.

In much the same way that the executive summary from a public inquiry can be used to highlight the salient points and actions, it can also be prudent to have summary reports that are targeted at diverse groups of people, whether internal or external.

When making the decision to share information externally, be aware of the level of redaction that may be utilized and whether this gives rise to the question that the organization is trying to hide something. If information needs to be removed or altered for legal or privacy reasons, it is better to highlight this and the reasons why rather than leave gaps in reports. Consider whether you can remove sensitive details, such as a person's name, rather than entire sections. This means that the spirit and context of the report remain intact whilst respecting privacy or other specific needs.

If making recommendations and assigning actions, these need to be tracked to fruition, with periodic updates, on the closure of each action. Do not assume that just because you have assigned an action, the recipient understands the action or has the skills and resources to enact the action.

Similarly, if the actions do not get performed, or are delayed, are there any repercussions? Is there a risk that the incident will reoccur, and will things get worse?

Pay attention to the fact that as time goes by, the impetus to fix underlying issues or change processes may reduce, people may change roles, and there will inevitably be other things that take priority, so the actions or risks move further down the list, until they may fall off the list completely.

If a subsequent or more serious incident occurs as a result of the inability or desire to systematically close actions, this will be identified in any subsequent investigation or inquiry.

As we identified in *Chapter 2, Action*, every action, or inaction has a potential consequence or knock-on effect, so it is prudent to highlight the repercussions upfront so that there is no ambiguity on what you are asking people to do and why.

Conclusion

In this chapter, I have discussed the importance and timeliness of performing investigations. We explored the array of opportunities that we have to learn from public inquiries and how such investigations may need to be performed in phases to get a good understanding and appreciation of the '*how*' and '*why*' incidents occur.

Reflection

- What was your impression of the case study in terms of how major changes are implemented, tested, and exercised?

- What is the frequency of change in your organization, and are you aware of major changes to business models and physical or technical infrastructure that may change or alter the integrity of the incident and crisis response?

- How are people made aware that the actions and information that they made be reliant on have changed or may no longer be fit for purpose?

- When you receive actions, audit logs, change records, system updates, test results, and so on., do you verify the accuracy and legitimacy of the information provided? Is it hearsay speculation or based on factual evidence?

- Consider the reliance that people may have on the reports and what decisions and actions people are expected to take because of reading them. As I discussed in *Chapter 2, Believable,* what are the consequences of inaction verse no action, and is there an opportunity to go back and review the decision(s) later to determine if they are still valid?

- When considering the need to perform a post-incident review or investigation, are you involving independent third parties, and are your actions helping or hindering them?

Suggested actions

- As well as those actions highlighted in the case, think back to what I spoke about in chapter 2 in terms of the need to record all actions for subsequent review and investigation. These need to be collated from each action owner and decision maker to form a chronological timeline and factual record of events leading up to and during the incident. Determine if there are conflicts on timelines and actions that need to be investigated to see how actions were time-dated and collaborated. For you cannot investigate the '*Why*' until you have established the '*How*' and '*When.*'

- Create a central command and control function for managing major incidents. This should not only be set up when an incident is in situ but should be in place to actively manage the incident and crisis management response in preparation for an incident. For larger enterprises, this may necessitate a physical room or center, and for small organizations, this can simply be a centralized phone number, email address, and repository that makes it easy for people to report and communicate with the incident and crisis responder(s). Symbolically, it can also help people to feel safe, knowing that such a function is in situ.

- Ensure that there is a central record of all major incidents and crisis reports and these can be easily accessed and retrieved. Consider whether there is a mechanism that allows for recording the type of incident and for searching on key terms for ease of correlation.

In the next chapter, I shall explore the subject of 'Justice'. This coincides nicely with this chapter, as there is often a tendency to want to look for someone to blame following an investigation. I will discuss why this can have a negative effect and why it doesn't yield the necessary outcomes.

CHAPTER 11
Justice

J = JUSTICE

"All the great things are simple, and many can be expressed in a single word: freedom, justice, honor, duty, mercy, hope."

—*Winston Churchill, Former U.K. Prime Minister*

The concept of justice is another widely debated subject that covers several social, ethical, moral, cultural, and legal issues.

At the core is the premise of the fundamental right to fairness and equity irrespective of a person's social standing or circumstance. The concept of innocent until proven guilty and the right to defend themselves.

Article 7 of the United Nations '*Universal Declaration of Human Rights*[1]' (1948) states that:

"*All are equal before the law and are entitled without any discrimination to equal protection of the law. All are entitled to equal protection against any discrimination in violation of this Declaration and against any incitement to such discrimination.*"

So where am I going with this?

Structure

In this chapter, I will discuss-

- Apportioning blame
- Dealing with negligence
- Case study 3: Colonial Pipeline ransomware attack
- Miscarriages of justice

Objectives

The aim of this chapter is to ensure that when faced with a major incident or crisis, we are not quick to jump to conclusions and apportion blame when things go wrong. I shall explore the issues of negligence as we take a look at our next case study. It is imperative that we are mindful of our approach and understand the consequences of our actions when seeking justice.

Apportioning blame

Quite often, I hear people referred to as the weakest link or they are labeled as repeat offenders, especially in the context of cybersecurity.

We are quick to apportion blame without evidence, or we reaffirm stereotypes through the language and unconscious bias we have attributed to people. We have automatically assumed a level of intent or guilt that may not be justified.

---

1 Article 7, Universal Declaration of Human Rights, United Nations (first published 10 December 1948): https://www.un.org/en/about-us/universal-declaration-of-human-rights, retrieved 1 July 2022

There is a tendency to want to blame a single person or entity, to look for a scapegoat when things go wrong, or to want to close the incident and move on quickly. It is a way of avoiding the subject in a vain attempt that no one notices.

So, why are people quick to want to judge or apportion blame?

Some of this can be down to social, cultural, moral, or religious beliefs and values, in how people perceive what is just and right, or how things occur.

Some people may find it difficult to introspect and instead project this onto others. Leveraging emotional intelligence and the principles of being fair and just is important when helping people to reflect rather than deflect.

Some people may also be of the mindset that the individual or organization brought it on themselves and should be punished or held to account.

This is particularly evident in the case of a cyberattack, where organizations are so focused on attribution and identifying the perpetrator(s) of the attack or data breach that they lose focus on what gave rise to the attack in the first place and what *'Lessons'* can be learned from this.

You may consider that dismissing a person(s) within the organization may bring closure to the situation, but if this has not been thoroughly investigated, it may give rise to cases for unfair dismissal or disgruntled employees that either post things on social media and other channels, or other employees come out in their favor.

Simply dismissing a person(s) for negligence or inappropriate behavior does nothing to improve the underlying reason that gave rise to the incident occurring in the first place or what steps are required to improve processes and educate people on new and changing practices.

As identified previously with issues with culture, if the organization is quick to apportion blame, and has a history of dismissing employees, then other employees will be more hesitant to admit that they have made a mistake or identified an issue. So rather than fix the problem, it may exasperate the issue further.

Of course, disciplinary action or dismissal may be a valid action, but it is one that requires careful consideration when the company is experiencing a crisis. This can also give rise to further grievances or acts of whistleblowing, as discussed in the previous chapter.

Dealing with negligence

In *Chapter 5 Diligence,* we discussed the importance of having a duty of care when identifying issues with defective products and services and the duty of care that organizations have in establishing the reliability, safety, and security of those products and services.

Dependent on the nature of the incident, there may be a criminal investigation, prosecutions, fines, and demands for compensation. This can also lead to civil action, or class action lawsuits, dependent on the country, because of claims of negligence against the organization or individuals involved.

In the next case study, we shall look at an example of where two class action complaints were brought by multiple plaintiffs, citing negligence in how the organization had prepared for and managed the response to a cyberattack that caused a ripple effect across the operational network and supply chain.

At the time of this book's publication, the lawsuits and evidence were still being collated and have yet to be concluded. It may be several years before the outcome of the lawsuits and other criminal or civil actions is known.

In addition, a *U.S. Congress Select Committee* also called into question the legitimacy of paying a ransom without involving federal authorities and whether the organization had adequate contingency plans for such an event.

Case study 3

Case Study 3
Colonial Pipeline Ransomware Attack
USA, 2021
Summary of incident
On 7th May 2021, Colonial Pipeline, a U.S. oil pipeline that carries gasoline and jet fuel, suffered a ransomware cyberattack.
The Colonial Pipeline is a critical part of the U.S. petroleum infrastructure, transporting c.100 million gallons of gasoline, diesel fuel, heating oil, and jet fuel per day. The pipeline stretches 5,500 miles and carries half of the East Coast's fuel supply.
In response to the ransomware attack, the organization halted all the pipeline's operations to contain the attack. The company initially said[2] this was because its billing system was compromised, and they were concerned they would not be able to figure out how much to bill customers for fuel they received
Colonial Pipeline paid the requested ransom (75 bitcoin or $ 4.4 million) within several hours after the extortion demand was made.

---

2 Natasha Bertrand, Evan Perez, Zachary Cohen, Geneva Sands and Josh Campbell, CNN News, 13 May 2021, https://edition.cnn.com/2021/05/12/politics/colonial-pipeline-ransomware-payment/index.html (retrieved 27 July 2022)

Once paid, the ransomware operators sent Colonial Pipeline a software application to restore their network, but the decryption software operated very slowly, and it did not fully recover services. The CEO told *The Wall Street Journal*[3] that he authorized the ransom payment because executives were unsure how badly the cyberattack had breached its systems or how long it would take to bring the pipeline back, which appeared to be a different reason than first given. This led some people to speculate about the decision made.

The decision to close the pipeline led to severe fuel shortages across seven airports, which led to low fuel alerts being issued by several airlines. At least two flights had fuel stops or plane changes added to their schedules for a four-day period. The shortage also required Atlanta International Airport to use other fuel suppliers.

Diesel and petroleum shortages began to occur at filling stations amid panic buying by the public as the pipeline shutdown entered its fourth day, with 71% of filling stations running out of fuel in Charlotte and 87% of stations in Washington, D.C. Average U.S. fuel prices rose to their highest point since 2014, reaching more than $3 a gallon.

As Colonial prepared to restore services following a six-day shutdown, personnel patrolled the pipeline, searching for any signs of physical damage. They dispatched three hundred workers to keep their eyes on the pipeline, supplementing its usual electronic monitoring.

The ransomware attack was the largest publicly disclosed cyberattack on an oil infrastructure target in the history of the U.S. The *Federal Bureau of Investigation* (*FBI*)[4] identified the Russian criminal group *DarkSide* as the responsible party. The same group is believed to have stolen one hundred gigabytes of data from company servers the day before the cyberattack.

On 7 June 2021, the *Department of Justice* announced[5] that it had recovered 63.7 of the bitcoins (approximately $2.3 million) from the ransom payment. Through possession of the private key of the ransom account, the FBI was able to retrieve the bitcoin though it did not disclose how it obtained the private key.

---

3 Collin Eaton and Dustin Volz, Colonial Pipeline CEO Tells Why He Paid Hackers a $4.4 Million Ransom, 19 May 2022, https://www.wsj.com/articles/colonial-pipeline-ceo-tells-why-he-paid-hackers-a-4-4-million-ransom-11621435636 (retrieved 27 July 2022)

4 FBI National Press Office, FBI Statement on Compromise of Colonial Pipeline Networks, 10 May 2021: https://www.fbi.gov/news/press-releases/press-releases/fbi-statement-on-compromise-of-colonial-pipeline-networks (retrieved 27 July 2022)

5 Department of Justice, Office of Public Affairs, Department of Justice Seizes $2.3 Million in Cryptocurrency Paid to the Ransomware Extortionists Darkside, 7 June 2021: https://www.justice.gov/opa/pr/department-justice-seizes-23-million-cryptocurrency-paid-ransomware-extortionists-darkside (retrieved 28 July 2022)

Analysis of the incident

The decision to pay the ransom within hours of the demand, coupled with the decision to close the pipeline, despite there being no evidence of an operational impact, attracted much media and public backlash

- On 18th May 2021, a class action complaint[6] was filed in Georgia, by over one hundred plaintiffs, from multiple U.S. states. The complaint cited that *"The Defendant's failure to properly secure the Colonial Pipeline's critical infrastructure – left it subjected to potential ransomware attacks like the one that took place on May 7, 2021 – leading to catastrophic effects for consumers and other end-users of gasoline up and down the east coast".*

- In addition, *"The Defendant's unlawfully deficient data security has injured millions of consumers in the form of higher gas prices, and gasoline shortages that exist/existed, due to Colonial's decision to effectively turn off the Pipeline. As a result, Plaintiff brings this action to redress the injuries caused to them and the members of the proposed Class due to Defendant's conduct."*

- A further class action complaint[7] was filed on 21 June 2021 by a law firm operating on behalf of the 11,000 gas stations negatively impacted by the shutdown, causing a sharp increase in the price of gasoline for automobiles and other motor vehicles and a sharp decrease in convenience store sales. The complaint claims that *"Defendant disregarded the rights of Plaintiff and Class Members by intentionally, willfully, recklessly, or negligently failing to take and implement adequate and reasonable measures to ensure that the Pipeline's critical infrastructure was safeguarded."*

- Due to the amount of publicity in the media, and obvious concerns from consumers, the email protection firm *Inky*[8], identified a series of follow-on cyberattacks from opportunists, utilizing a fake Help Desk site to contact

---

6 Complaint-Class Action Demand for Jury Trial, Dickerson verses CPDQ Colonial Partners, Case 1:21-cv-02098-MHC, filed Northern District of Georgia, 18 May 2021, https://www.classaction.org/media/dickerson-v-cdpq-colonial-partners-lp-et-al.pdf (retrieved 10 July 2022)

7 Complaint-Class Action Demand for Jury Trial, EZ Mart LLC verses Colonial Pipeline Company, Case No: 1:21-cv-02522, filed Northern District of Georgia, 21 June 2021, https://www.classaction.org/media/ez-mart-1-llc-v-colonial-pipeline-company.pdf (retrieved 15 July 2022)

8 Roger Kay, Inky Security Blog, June 2021, https://www.inky.com/en/blog/colonial-pipeline-ransomware-hack-unleashes-flood-of-related-phishing-attempts (retrieved 21 July 2022)

Colonial's customers. These attacks were based on two factors – 1) the Colonial ransomware attack itself and 2) the public availability of a highly effective remote-access tool. Attackers tried to exploit consumer anxiety, offering them a software update that would *"fix"* the problem via a highly targeted email. All the recipients had to do was click a button to enable the update. However, by clicking the button in the email, it launched malware onto the recipient's device, which would enable the attacker to obtain remote access to the device or systems.

- On 9th June 2021, a hearing was held before the *U.S. Congress Committee on Homeland Security*, which focused on learning lessons[9] from the Colonial Pipeline to protect critical infrastructure. The transcripts from the Committee highlighted:

  - *"Fundamental questions need to be raised about the cybersecurity practices of critical infrastructure owners and operators and whether voluntary cybersecurity standards are sufficient to defend against today's cyber threat"*.

  - The Committee highlighted that the private sector operates 85% of U.S. critical infrastructure, and much of it has some connectivity to the internet. The vulnerabilities in computing technology, from the most complex systems to the smallest devices, are often found in its software.

  Committee's comments on paying ransoms and how this fuels terrorist networks and organized crime:

  - *"There is a need to break the ransomware business model. We cannot accept the default to accepting extortion."*

  - *"Paying a ransom emboldens and encourages bad actors and places everyone at greater risk for the financial and societal costs of increases in threats as others seek payouts."*

  - *"If there is silence about cyberattacks like ransomware, the criminals and terrorists will remain out of reach and continue to feel safe in carrying out these attacks."*

  - *"The ill-gotten gain reaped from ransomware can be used to fuel terrorist networks, drug cartels, attacks against the homeland, human trafficking, or other efforts to undermine homeland security."*

---

9 U.S. House of Representatives, Committee on Homeland Security, 'Cyber Threats in the Pipeline: Using lessons from the Colonial Pipeline Attack of Defend Critical Infrastructure', First Session, (9 June 2021): https://www.congress.gov/event/117th-congress/house-event/LC66855/text (retrieved 10 July 2022)

Comments relating to the CEO's decision to pay the ransom:

- o The CEO stated that following consultation with outside legal representation, they made the decision to proceed with negotiations with the criminal actor. There was no discussion with the FBI or any governmental entity about the ransom or negotiation – it was a two-day gap between when the ransom was paid, and the FBI was informed

- o The CEO stated: *"I made the decision to pay, and I made the decision to keep the information about the payment as confidential as possible…I kept the information closely held because we were concerned about operational security, and we wanted to stay focused on getting the pipeline back up and running."*

- o *"I want to emphasize that the importance of protecting critical infrastructure drove the decision to halt operations of the pipeline to help ensure that the malware was not able to spread to our OT network."*

- o *"We did not know the point of origination of the attack nor the scope of it, so bringing the entire system down was the surest way--and the right way--to contain any potential damage."*

- o The CEO was asked to confirm whether he expected Colonial's insurance company to cover the ransom payment, in which he inferred that a claim had been submitted after the fact, although it is not clear whether the firm was consulted prior to paying the ransom demand, or whether this was subsequently paid.

Comments relating to the recovery effort:

- o Although a software decrypter was provided by the threat actor following the payment of the ransom, it did not work effectively, and there were bugs in it. The CEO stated that, in the end, it was not needed to recover systems.

- o The Committee highlighted that if the organization already had the capacity to get back online through backups – why did they pay the ransom, and why did they disconnect the pipeline? The CEO responded that: *"I availed myself of an option that, in hindsight, we didn't necessarily need, but we wouldn't have known it for days, which would have just delayed our ability to start the system back up."*

Comments relating to how attackers got access:

- o   Forensic investigator *Mandiant* who was brought in by Colonial after the ransomware attack identified that the attacker was able to exploit an unprotected Virtual Private Network (VPN) account that was no longer in use to gain access to Colonial Pipeline's network.

- o   Whilst the password being utilized was strong, it had been found in use on other websites. The account had potentially been compromised several days prior to the ransom demand.

Comments relating to the recovery strategy and testing of response plans:

- o   The CEO advised that they did not have a specific ransomware strategy but a generic emergency response plan.

- o   The Committee asked why the organization had not participated in some of the independent testing provided through government agencies, to which the CEO stated that they participate in many *'tabletop exercises'* and that there are standards that they follow.

- o   When questioned, the CEO agreed with the need for more security penetration testing for organizations, to test the defenses, and to test their assumptions with respect to controls that they believe they have.

Committee general comments on U.S. cyber defenses relating to the protection of critical infrastructure:

- o   *"It is deeply concerning that Russian hackers, through a compromised password on a virtual proxy network, were able to essentially shut down a 5,500-mile pipeline."*

- o   *"The attack on Colonial demonstrates the need to shore up cyber defenses through initiatives such as public-private partnerships."*

- o   *"Continuity planning is also firmly under the control of organizations, and to not invest in proven strategies to survive a cyber-attack, is not only irresponsible on the part of owners--but it creates unacceptable risks for their employees, customers, and investors."*

- o   *"More work must be done to secure critical infrastructure from cybersecurity vulnerabilities that include oil and gas pipelines, the electric and grid, and water treatment facilities. This is especially critical to the protection of large complex information systems that run on applications and hardware that may be decades old."*

Lessons we can learn from this:

- Organizations require a clear *'Strategy'* on ransomware, which considers the full consequences of paying versus not paying an extortion demand. This should consider more than just whether it will get services back quicker, but also considers the social, legal, and ethical dilemmas associated with funding organized crime.

- Since extortion and blackmail are both criminal offenses, this is not something that an organization should do in isolation and requires input and guidance from law enforcement. Once money has been extorted, it is quickly moved and laundered across jurisdictions, which makes attribution and prosecution more difficult. Organizations should consider having a single point of contact for law enforcement as part of the crisis response strategy. This includes proactive engagement to remove any misunderstandings and ambiguities about the role that law enforcement has, and the support they will provide during an active cyberattack.

- Of note in this scenario, is that the organization could not have performed a deep enough *'Investigation'* of the services impacted, or not impacted by the encryption, before a decision to pay was made. This is an essential element in determining *'Facts,'* and what information is needed to verify any assumptions being made. The CEO also made potentially conflicting statements on reasons for why the ransom was paid – citing to the Wall Street Journal that it was due to the inability to bill consumers, and to the U.S. Congress that it was to protect the operational network. The reasons and rationale for decisions need to be clear and unambiguous, as we discussed under *'Actions,'* even if that decision is later confirmed as being incorrect or unfounded.

- As identified by Colonial themselves, and similar to other ransomware attacks, decryption keys provided by attackers are often full of bugs, corrupt or unusable. Each file needs to be recovered one at a time, and this can be time-consuming, assuming files can even be recovered at all.

- Ransomware attackers may utilize a *'double extortion'* model, whereby the first extortion request is for a decryption key, and the second extortion request is to stop the release of exfiltrated data.

- With an assume compromise mindset, you should consider that exfiltrated files have already been sold on dark web markets, and that copies will have been taken, to be used for secondary attacks.

- that enable organizations to rebuild and restore services without paying ransom demands. It is also important to take steps to evict the attacker from the organization's networks to prevent further reconnaissance and attacks from being performed.

- The information in the transcript with U.S. Congress, also highlighted a lack of awareness by the CEO of two things that could have changed the trajectory of the incident at the outset:

  1. Information on retained services and expert forensics, which may have been readily available to the organization at time of incident, to identify the extent of the compromise on operational networks.

  2. Understanding of the current state of backups, and how long it would have taken to perform a full rebuild of impacted services, potentially negating the need to negotiate payment for the decryption key.

- When examining how attackers got access to the network, this identified common and preventable issues with passwords – that is sharing and reusing passwords across multiple websites and systems. Whilst the password itself was sufficiently complex, it had been utilized elsewhere which enabled the attacker to find out how many other services they could open. Strategies for identity and access management are critical to preventing the initial stages of cyberattacks. This is also a core component of designing '*Zero Trust*' architectures.

- As with many organizations that manage critical infrastructure, there is an increasing need to integrate IT (information technology) and OT (operational technology) networks. Arguably many attackers have a much deeper understanding of IT infrastructure than OT environments.

  The payment of ransoms enables attackers to procure specialist resources, which have the knowledge and expertise to infiltrate and sabotage these environments, which can also include the deliberate targeting of insiders. Attackers have come to learn that there are higher stakes, and ransoms available by disrupting OT networks. The danger is that this could lead to a wide-scale industrial accident, if not handled and managed effectively.

- There is a need to balance the criticality and impact of loss of services, with investment levels. Often cybersecurity and resilience functions are seen as cost centers, but these areas are increasingly fundamental to the reputation and trust that consumers have in organizations.

- Whilst it is impractical to suggest that organizations can remove all vulnerabilities, they should determine how these can be exploited, and have contingency plans to reduce the probability or impact of a major incident, and to also ensure that management is fully aware, and conversant of the risks and implications.

- A key area of debate has also risen in terms of the role that insurance companies play in increasing both the probability of extortion demands, and the likelihood of a payout being made by an insurer, rather than the organization itself. Often the ransomware operators have performed enough reconnaissance on their targets to determine whether a) they have cyber insurance, and b) the value of any potential payout.

This can influence the value of the ransom demand, as well as the aggressive demands placed upon the organization to influence the outcome. The sharp rise in ransom payments and payouts has led some insurers and underwriters to suspend or restrict payments[10], and to seek clarity from law enforcement and regulators on whether payment of ransoms will be outlawed.

The fear is that doing so, effectively penalizes and criminalizes the victims, rather than the perpetrators. What is clear is that cyber insurance is still being offered in the interim, but organizations should expect stricter conditions, when it comes to proving how they manage their overall security posture and risk, and that they are taking definitive action to manage the increased threat.

- A key aspect of this book, and why it was written evolves around '*Lessons*' and '*Knowledge*' – this means sharing intelligence and information on different threat actors, evolving tactics utilized by attackers, and techniques that organizations can deploy to reinforce and harden their defenses. As the Colonial CEO himself stated in his evidence to U.S. Congress: "*I am sure there is any number of reasons why people are hesitant to it, they are embarrassed, they have a brand name they are trying to protect. But I think eventually transparency and honesty are extremely important in our effort to try to stop what we are seeing become a daily event increasingly.*"

- Another common misconception that can often happen in a cyberattack is that if I have been attacked once, I won't be attacked again, which is incorrect. Often when attackers have got access to the corporate network and infrastructure, information and data are collated to enable follow-on or subsequent attacks. As I mentioned in the Introduction, there has been a significant increase in the role of '*access brokers*' in buying and selling information on dark web markets that would enable other attackers to launch other attacks. Organizations need to continue to remain vigilant following an attack and should not be complacent,

10 Josephine Wolff, Wired, 'As Ransomware Demands Boom, Insurance Companies Keep Paying Out', 12 June 2021, https://www.wired.com/story/ransomware-insurance-payments (retrieved 26 July 2022)

Whether a major incident has been caused by accident or because of deliberate action, such as a cyberattack, often this only occurs because of underpinning vulnerabilities and gaps in processes.

Formal investigations or inquiries can take several years and have a major impact on reputation. This could have additional consequences where the organization is seeking investment, mergers, and acquisitions, as such investigations may need to be declared to potential shareholders and investors.

This can be drawn out and have dire consequences if the organization has tried to hide, alter, or remove information.

Miscarriages of justice

Sometimes an organization can be so convinced of the guilt of a specific perpetrator(s) that they seek out information or accept information as *'Facts'* where it reinforces their own conscious or unconscious biases. Often ignoring or downplaying the information that did not fit with the rhetoric.

It is important, therefore, that when seeking justice, we are not quick to jump to conclusions and are mindful and questioning each source of information, and how this may help or hinder the case.

Also, consider the detriment to the organization and / or individuals if a miscarriage of justice has occurred and whether this gives rise to claims for further claims of compensation, lawsuits, and even prosecution.

If we are mindful and systematic in our approach, we can enable positive change and better outcomes for all. This requires being open-minded, even if the outcome and findings do not benefit the organization.

This brings to bare the topics on *'Diligence,' 'Empathy,' 'Facts,' 'Honesty,'* and *'Investigation,'* that we have explored in previous chapters, and highlights why these topics are inter-related and are important factors when considering the end-to-end strategy for incident response and crisis management.

Conclusion

In this chapter, I have discussed the subject of justice and why it covers several social, ethical, moral, cultural, and legal issues. When we are quick to jump to conclusions or apportion blame, it can have negative consequences if such claims are unfounded or not based on *'Facts.'* We have discussed how the mishandling of an incident can also give rise to claims of negligence, which can compound the situation further.

Reflection

- What was your impression of the case study and how Colonial Pipeline responded in the initial hours and days of the attack?

- Thinking back to *Chapter 5, 'Diligence'*, what process is in place for establishing justice when the organization has been found to be negligent or where there are claims for civil or criminal action?

- What independent testing and verification are you performing to substantiate organizational claims that infrastructure is safe, secure, and reliable?

Suggested actions

- Thinking back to the action plan in *Chapter 2, Action*, and communication strategy in *Chapter 4, Communication*, ensure that insurers and outside legal counsel are involved in the incident response to verify some of the decisions and actions that are being made by the organization.

- In case of suspected, or confirmed criminal activity, ensure that law enforcement is included in the incident response and advice is sought where possible. It is prudent to liaise with law enforcement in advance of a major incident to aid in the training and awareness of key decision makers in the organization and so that they may provide guidance on the recommended response or help that can be provided by law enforcement, or other emergency services in a crisis.

In the next chapter, we explore the importance of sharing and collaboration in our pursuit of *'Knowledge'* and how we can be most effective at applying lessons.

CHAPTER 12
Knowledge

K = KNOWLEDGE

"Knowledge is power."

—Sir Francis Bacon, English Philosopher

This gives rise to the notion that sharing knowledge is the cornerstone of establishing a reputation and influences decision-making.

But what does that really mean, or how useful is knowledge if only retained by a handful of people and that information is not shared?

Simply having lots of information is pointless if we cannot extract the value from it or we do not know what *'Actions'* to take as a result.

So how do we use the resulting knowledge to benefit the masses?

Firstly, we need to know what it is we are looking for, how we can use it for the greater good, and how we can educate others to extract the value too.

The value only comes from how that knowledge is subsequently utilized. Our pursuit of knowledge can help with problem-solving and reaffirms our reasoning and the action we need to take.

Structure

In this chapter, I will discuss the following:

- Turning knowledge into intelligence
- Case study 4 – Russian invasion of Ukraine
- Education and Awareness
- Sharing and collaboration

Objectives

In this chapter, I shall explore why we need to extract intelligence from knowledge and why this only has value when it is fully utilized and acted upon. I shall discuss why sharing and collaboration have become imperative in the current threat landscape as we take a look at case study 4.

Turning knowledge into intelligence

Intelligence comes from knowing how and when to apply knowledge for the greatest impact, coupled with experience, ability, and judgment.

Intelligence pertaining to a nation-state and organized crime groups used to be held by government and intelligence agencies and was not readily available to many organizations. There is an appreciation that information and intelligence need to be put into the hands of those that need to consider critical infrastructure and ongoing supply of products and services – that includes private sector organizations.

The impact of war affects all nations, irrespective of geographical location, due to the volatility of stock markets and currency. This can cause inflation to rise and economies to crash into recession.

In the next case study, I will consider how physical attacks and cyberattacks are evolving, particularly in relation to nation-state actors. At the time of publication, the Russian invasion of Ukraine is still active. Therefore, the aim of the case study is not to discuss the specifics of the invasion but to explain why the need to share intelligence about evolving tactics and collaboration across the public-private sector has become pivotal.

We shall explore how kinetic and cyber warfare are combined and how '*information warfare*' is also being utilized in propaganda as another weapon to alter public perception. This is a sign of the digital era, where information can be easily shared and disseminated across the world in seconds.

The ease by which information can be propagated, and shared on social media, means that it has become awash with largely unsubstantiated claims, ideas, and solutions that aren't peer-reviewed and sources that aren't cited. We see people sharing '*intelligence*' or '*information*' on threats when this can be a breeding ground for misinformation and disinformation.

Case study 4

Case study 4
Russian Invasion
Ukraine, 2022
Summary of incident
On 24th February 2022, the Russian Federation launched an invasion of Ukraine.
Within minutes of the invasion, the Russian military launched multiple cruise missile attacks from the air and sea, as explosions were reported in several Ukraine cities. Russian soldiers on the ground advanced from several locations within Russia, Belarus, and Crimea.
Not only did the Russian government launch missile attacks against the Ukraine military, government, and critical infrastructure, but they also discriminately targeted civilians, including functioning hospitals, which is regarded as a crime under the terms of Article 3 of the *Geneva Convention*[1] with focuses on the need for humanitarian aid during times of conflict, and support for injured military personnel and citizens, irrespective of country.

1 International Committee of the Red Cross, the Geneva Conventions of 1949 and their Additional Protocols, 29 October 2019, https://www.icrc.org/en/doc/war-and-law/treaties-customary-law/geneva-conventions/overview-geneva-conventions.htm (retrieved 29 July 2022)

At the same time, Russia also launched simultaneous and highly targeted cyberattacks with precision. These were timed to correspond with kinetic attacks as a way of crippling Ukraine's infrastructure, impacting its ability to respond as quickly and efficiently as possible.

Analysis of the incident

- The war in Ukraine is an example of a *hybrid war*[2], which consists of a well-organized military, diplomatic, economic, and media campaign. This is aimed at defeating the target country swiftly by breaking its ability to resist an attack without the need to launch a full-scale military attack. It is designed as a means of getting the target country to surrender quickly.

- This tactic was observed in 2014, during the previous Russian invasion of Ukraine and the annexation of the Crimea peninsula. *The Finish Institute of International Affairs* highlighted that part of the tactics of the hybrid war involves exploiting weaknesses at all levels – not just in infrastructure, but any dissatisfaction or indifference from the public aimed at government groups or policies. This can also include marginalized and religious groups.

- Although similar tactics are being utilized in the current war, this has evolved to include a much higher emphasis on cyber and electronic warfare as a means of knocking out communications channels as early as possible and using cyberattacks to establish persistence.

- Whilst the physical invasion happened on February 24th, 2022. The first cyberattacks were fired the day before against nineteen government and critical infrastructure entities. The aim of this was to try and limit Ukraine's ability to respond.

- A *Microsoft* report[3], which examined the early lessons from the war, highlighted the sophisticated coordination of Russia's cyber operations, both inside and outside Ukraine. This focuses on three areas:

⇒ **Destructive cyberattacks**

Utilizing targeted phishing campaigns to gain access to target computer networks.

Planting malware designed to *"wipe"* computer hard disks and destroy all data. The malware architecture is designed to replicate or spread malware to other computers across a network of an entire government ministry.

However, unlike the NotPetya[4] cyberattacks in 2017, which started in Ukraine and quickly spread globally, the malware was designed to stay within the target network.

⇒ **Cyber Espionage outside Ukraine**

As a coalition of countries came together to defend Ukraine through military assistance and sanctions on Russia, the Russian intelligence agencies stepped up their network penetration and espionage activities targeting governments outside Ukraine.

⇒ **Cyber influence**

Using digital technologies and the internet to create and spread false narratives to advance political goals. These are designed to have a broad geographic reach, delivered in high volumes with precise targeting. This was observed against four key audiences:

1. The Russian population, with the aim of sustaining support for the invasion.

2. The Ukrainian population undermined confidence in the government.

3. The U.S., and European populations, undermine Western unity.

4. Non-aligned countries, to gain more support for Russian efforts.

Lessons we can learn from this

o The Russian invasion of Ukraine has highlighted how advances in digital technology and infrastructure have enabled a new wave of attacks that, when combined, work in unison to cause long-term damage.

o It has also highlighted that in times of conflict and during a crisis, the protection of digital infrastructure and communications is also essential. Those aimed at civilian populations and organizations, such as TV broadcasting stations, the internet, and social media, as mechanisms for disseminating information. It is vital, however, that people understand how to decipher the '*Facts*' from fiction and the dangers of accessing and sharing information from untrusted sources.

o Hybrid warfare is deemed successful because the attacker can perform reconnaissance and identify weaknesses that can be exploited. This can be weaknesses in physical and digital infrastructure and public and employee perception, which can all be exploited. The more gaps that exist, the more attackers can take advantage of this.

o Having good governance and visibility across disparate areas is essential for understanding how these weaknesses can lead to failure or compromise, and so critical infrastructure needs to be protected from sabotage.

> o As I explored previously when looking at issues with disinformation in *Chapter 7, Facts* establishing good governance relies on having a culture that respects human rights and provides transparency to enable people to build their own knowledge and take necessary actions? Furthermore, and as highlighted, disinformation campaigns can come from multiple sources and not just nation-state actors. It is why I highlighted it as a growing threat in the age of digital communications.
>
> o In *Chapter 14, Media,* I highlight why freedom of expression and preventing censorship are key in preventing marginalized groups from being actively targeted.

Education and awareness

A key tenet of knowledge is education and awareness. For many organizations, awareness has become synonymous with compliance, where success is measured in how many people took a training course or passed a test. As we discussed in *Chapter 4, Communication,* are we making sure there is a clear understanding of required actions, and is the awareness really for the benefit of the people, or is it for the benefit of the organization?

The reality is that this should be both to be truly effective. Organizations, therefore, need to consider the intended outcomes and behaviors as a measure of the education provided. This means asking '*Questions*' about the value that education and awareness are providing and whether they truly embody knowledge.

There is a difference between simply building awareness and building understanding. The former is about perception, whereas the latter is about gaining knowledge and understanding why.

Simply being aware of a subject does little to change behaviors, so there needs to be mechanisms in place that can measure and evaluate the outcome of the awareness and education and how this enables people to change their mindset and be more cognizant of the requirements or actions, that is expected of them.

Sharing and collaboration

Education and awareness are essential for building knowledge within the organization, but the full benefit comes from when we share and collaborate externally. This provides education on the knowledge and intelligence that has been gathered to enable others to learn, refine and continually improve their understanding and the applicability of that knowledge.

This is how we truly enable the power of knowledge by turning this into actionable intelligence that benefits all. If we restrict the level of knowledge that is shared internally or externally to the organization, we potentially miss information, which reduces the efficacy of the *'Investigation'* and *'Lessons'* that can be applied, especially when trying to avoid repeat incidents within the same or other organizations.

Often organizations retain a lot of knowledge and intelligence that they have gathered from multiple sources that are publicly available, but that needs to extend that information and knowledge that has not been shared to get the full impact. As I explored in the case study on the Colonial Pipeline ransomware attack, there is often an unwillingness to openly share information due to embarrassment or the stigma attached to becoming the victim of an attack, so this requires more public-private collaboration to share in an environment that promotes information sharing in a way that does not expose vulnerabilities to those that want to use the information for nefarious purposes.

Whilst there will always be considerations on the sensitivity and sharing of the information and how that is performed, there is also the need to consider the value that information has in reinforcing end-to-end resilience at an economic level.

The challenge today is that there is such a wealth of information, whether from legitimate or untrusted sources, that it can be difficult for organizations to decipher the relevancy of that information and its value of it. Simply having more intelligence does not help if we do not know how to apply it.

It is worth highlighting that our brains are not designed for multitasking, and we can get decision fatigue when dealing with more than 7-8 decision factors at a time. It drains our energy, and hence people can be prone to mistakes. This is why we discussed the need to create decision trees as part of the action plan in *Chapter 2, 'Action.'* This can help people to put things in perspective and to understand what is or is not in their control and what decisions they can make.

Psychologist *Daniel Kahneman*[5] believes that we tend to have two modes of thought:

⇒ Fast, instinctive, and emotional

⇒ Slow, deliberate, and logical

Whilst both can have their benefits in different situations, the second mode of thought enables us to think more rationally in a crisis. A lack of training or a defined action plan can mean that we are forced to perhaps react irrationally and instinctively and on our own intuition. We are more likely to make impulsive decisions rather than one that is well-considered and considers the consequences, as well as the next steps.

As we have seen in previous case studies, the inability to correlate information from multiple sources has been a major factor in many of the major incidents, and hence

---

5 Daniel Kahneman, Thinking Fast and Slow, 2011

organizations should consider how they can reduce the manual effort in collating and analyzing information from multiple sources.

The use of digital technology and infrastructure is not only critical for communications and information sharing, but it is also critical for extracting insights. Applying data analytics and machine learning algorithms to large disparate datasets enables organizations to look for patterns and relationships to correlate information from data sources.

Open-source researcher, *Bellingcat* [6] highlights how machine learning and artificial intelligence provide optimism in the ability to apply learning independently to process large datasets, which can identify anomalies in data that people may not be able to detect. This needs to be combined with human ingenuity to enable deep problem-solving now and into the future.

Extracting the value from knowledge and intelligence is an important aspect of informing current and future '*Strategy*.'.

Conclusion

In this chapter, I have explored why knowledge is power when utilized to the full effect. The true value of intelligence is gained from sharing and collaboration. When armed with the right information and facts, we are able to make better informed and rational decisions, which is vital in a crisis.

Reflection

- What is the organization's overall stance on gathering and sharing intelligence? How does this influence the overall approach to establishing and demonstrating '*Resilience*'?

- How is this level of intelligence shared inside and outside the organization, and how does this contribute to the knowledge that people need to make effective decisions?

- What is the organization's overall approach to governance, risk, and compliance when it comes to identifying, reporting, and managing vulnerabilities?

---

6 Eliot Higgins, We Are Bellingcat, An intelligence agency for people, 17 February 2022

Suggested actions

- Thinking back to the actions and decisions that people need to make throughout the incident and crisis management lifecycle, create a knowledge and skills matrix that identifies what knowledge is required to fulfill a role or task and how this is demonstrated.

- Consider how education and knowledge are measured. This needs to include how people can actively demonstrate their knowledge and gaps in knowledge. One of the most effective ways is through immersive training, tests, and exercises.

In the next chapter, I shall explore the subject of learning *'Lessons'*. As humans, we tend to have a poor record when it comes to researching and learning from historical events and is destined to repeat them unless we enable proactive change.

CHAPTER 13
Lessons

How we manage an incident is just as important as the incident itself.

However, we tend to have a problem with learning and applying lessons from incidents, which means we are destined to repeat mistakes over and over.

Structure

In this chapter, I will discuss-

- Utilizing the power of hindsight and foresight

- The fallacy of black swan events

- Case study 5 – 9/11 terrorist attacks

- Importance of isomorphic learning

- Applying lessons

Objectives

The aim of this chapter is to consider why we need to break the cycle when it comes to learning lessons. Hindsight and foresight can be valuable tools if used correctly, as is our ability to learn from others. Major incidents rarely just happen. Typically,, there have been a series of warnings and missed opportunities, which is what we shall explore further in case study 5.

Utilizing the power of hindsight and foresight

Hindsight is a wonderful tool, but only if it is used to inform what is to come.

The key difference between hindsight and foresight is that hindsight enables us to look backward at what has already happened to gain *Knowledge*. With the power of hindsight, the outcome is already known, but with foresight, we do not yet know the outcome. This requires someone to make a judgment or a prediction on what a likely outcome may look like.

Some might say that this is a fool's errand, as it is not possible to predict the exact outcome of an incident, let alone how and when it will occur. So how much time and effort should be applied in both endeavors since I cannot change the past, and I cannot predict the future?

However, with the benefit of hindsight and knowledge, we have the power to change the trajectory of what may be on the horizon by deliberately changing course. This could be for the worse or better, dependent on the intent.

A key thing to consider is whether the knowledge of previous events materially changes the perception of those events or whether they are destined to happen anyway. They potentially become a self-fulfilling prophecy because we put so much attention into the events or the outcome that the probability of something happening goes up rather than down.

I would argue that the more information and the more informed we are, the more we can proactively influence the outcome. As we identified in *Chapter 7, Facts*, a key aspect of this is determining facts we know to be true and a correlation of information.

Often when presented with such information, the causation and effect may seem obvious, and the writing on the wall that an event would occur. However, it is only when we purposely act to bring multiple sources of information together that we can see such things. The tragedies that we have shown in the case studies generated such a public outcry for answers that formal inquiries were instigated, often at great expense, time, and resources.

It is what we do with that information and that newfound knowledge that is critically important for what we choose to do next.

The fallacy of black swan events

The definition of a black swan event is an event so rare and unexpected that we could not have predicted it would happen.

The black swan metaphor was first termed by *Nasser Nicholas Taleb* [1], a mathematical statistician, who argued that such events could only be rationalized after the fact with the benefit of hindsight. His theory centered on the disproportionate impact of high-profile events, which are beyond the realm of normal expectations, the difficulty of applying computational methods to predictability, and the individual and collective biases that people may have across diverse cultures and life experiences.

In some respects, I agree with Taleb's theory, in that he states that our aim is to build robustness to such events, but I disagree with one thing - I do not believe that an event can be so big that it could not have been predicted. Certainly, the benefit of hindsight is a powerful tool, but there is one thing that every event has in common – not one of them occurred randomly, and not one of them by chance.

Of course, we cannot determine the exact chain of events in advance, but as we have seen from the case studies and anecdotes in this book, there is enough information and evidence available from previous incidents to highlight what could happen if warning signs are ignored, or not taken seriously.

As I mentioned in the *Introduction*, one of the examples often cited as a black swan event is the 9/11 terrorist attack. I have chosen this event as the next case study as

---

1 Nasser Nicholas Taleb, The Black Swan: The Impact of the Highly Improbable (2007)

an example of why I believe black swan events to be a fallacy. Of course, you will have your own opinion on this, and I certainly encourage you to have an open mind based on your own experiences.

There is no doubt that there have been events in history that have been so large and so shocking that we struggle to comprehend how such an event could ever happen, especially when events are televised to an audience of millions worldwide as the events unfold live.

As we have explored with previous case studies, we must ask ourselves how bad it will get before we see major change – at a global level. Typically, this befalls a tragedy of the enormity of 9/11.

The aim of this case study is not to analyze the details of the incident itself but rather to highlight some of the events and warnings that led up to the incident as an example of how events can escalate and why the notion of a black swan event, could potentially be dangerous, as it infers that such an event cannot be planned for.

Case study 5

Case study 5
9/11 Terrorist Attacks
USA, 2001
Summary of incident
On 11th September 2001, the U.S. experienced the deadliest terrorist attack on U.S. soil in history[2].

Nineteen hijackers boarded four domestic flights and soon after take-off hijacked or attempted to hi-jack and take control of the planes, and fly them to the intended targets:

- The first plane was piloted into the North Tower of the *World Trade Center* in New York City at 08:46. At first, many observers mistook this to be a tragic accident.

- The second plane was piloted into the South Tower some 17 minutes later, leaving no doubt that this was a deliberate attack and no accident.

- The third plane struck the south side of the *Pentagon* in Washington D.C. at 09:37. At which time, the *Federal Aviation Authority* ordered a grounding of all aircraft, preventing any further planes from taking off across the whole of the U.S.

2 Peter.L.Bergen, Britannica, September 11 Attacks, https://www.britannica.com/event/September-11-attacks/The-attacks retrieved 23 July 2022

- The fourth plane, already in the air, crashed in the Pennsylvania countryside as the crew and passengers onboard the plane attempted to overpower the assailants. It is believed that the intended target may have been *The White House* and other federal buildings in Washington, D.C.

Tragically 2,753 people were killed in New York, 184 at the Pentagon, and 40 in Pennsylvania. Thousands more people were injured on the ground and in surrounding areas.

A further 415 emergency workers were killed following the collapse of both Towers in New York, as hundreds of people had rushed to the scene of the attacks. This area would later be commemorated with the '*Ground Zero*' memorial.

The U.S. *Central Intelligence Agency (CIA)* identified that the coordinated attacks were conducted by the militant Islamic group *al-Qaeda*, though no group initially claimed responsibility. In October 2004, the Leader of *al-Qaeda* allegedly claimed responsibility for the attacks in a videotaped confession.

The *9/11 Commission* was set up in 2002 by the U.S. President and U.S. Congress to investigate the circumstances of the terrorist attack. What ensued was an enormous effort and commitment by the U.S. government and allied nations to combat terrorism.

Congress quickly passed the USA Patriot Act 2001[3] within 45 days of the terrorist attacks, which significantly expanded the search and surveillance powers of the *Federal Bureau of Investigation (FBI)* and other law-enforcement agencies to track and intercept communications and deter potential acts of terrorism. Although initially supported by the public, questions have since been raised about the issues of privacy when it comes to the mass surveillance of citizens without probable cause.

Analysis of the incident

- In July 2004, the 9/11 Commission published its Report[4] in which they examined several aspects of the events that led up to the terrorist attack.

- The key operational planner behind the attack had previously stated that he had planned to blow up several American planes in Asia during the mid-nineties, a plot that failed but never faded.

---

3 H.R.3162 - Uniting and Strengthening America by Providing Appropriate Tools Required to Intercept and Obstruct Terrorism (USA PATRIOT ACT) Act of 2001, https://www.congress.gov/bill/107th-congress/house-bill/3162/text/enr retrieved 24 July 2022

4 The 9/11 Commission Report: Final Report of the National Commission on Terrorist Attacks Upon the United States, July 2004: https://www.govinfo.gov/content/pkg/GPO-911REPORT/pdf/GPO-911REPORT.pdf retrieved 24 July 2022

- In 1996, he presented a proposal to the leader of *al-Qaeda* that would involve training pilots who would crash hi-jacked planes on U.S. targets in New York and Washington D.C.

- This required organization at a global scale, with multiple cells working in unison across several countries to fund and coordinate the plot, including the training of commercial jet pilots.

- The 9/11 Commission Report identified valuable lessons in hindsight and foresight, citing that *"Hindsight can sometimes see the past clearly—with 20/20 vision. But the path of what happened is so brightly lit that it places everything else more deeply into shadow."*

- The report identified that a terrorist attack on U.S. soil had not been deemed a credible threat in the year 2000 Presidential Election, and terrorism was not an important topic for debate.

- The Commission Report provided a timeline of reports and warnings that had been published:

    o In 1995, a *National Intelligence Estimate* predicted future terrorist attacks against the U.S. It warned that the danger would increase over several years and specified several points of vulnerability relating to the White House, the Capitol, symbols of capitalism such as Wall Street, critical infrastructures such as power grids, areas where people congregate such as sports arenas, and civil aviation.

    o The greatest danger would come as *"transient groupings of individuals"* that lacked *"strong organization but rather are loose affiliations."* They operate *"outside traditional circles but have access to a worldwide network of training facilities and safe havens."*

    o In 1996–1997, the intelligence community received new information making clear that the leader of al-Qaeda had lists of specific targets and operational commanders. Also revealed was the militant groups' involvement in a series of other terrorist attacks.

    o In 1998, reports came in of a possible al-Qaeda plan to hijack a plane. The most prominent of these mentioned a plot to fly an explosives-laden aircraft into a U.S. city.

- o From 1998 to 2001, several intelligence papers were distributed relating to the al-Qaeda leader's political philosophy, his command of a global network, analysis of information from terrorists captured, and the evolving goals of the Islamist extremist movement. Many classified articles were prepared for the highest officials in government, even up to August 2001, that al-Qaeda was determined to strike the U.S.

- Despite this, the Commission Report identified that the U.S. intelligence agencies lacked a complete picture and strategic analysis of the threat, with conflicting statements on proportionality since statements have been made about the risk of hundreds of deaths rather than thousands.

- In addition, the report highlighted that the threat of using an aircraft as a weapon had not been widely considered. Despite previous reports of hijackings, and planes used as weapons, this was not monitored, and correlations with previous threat reports from other agencies had not been made.

- The report highlighted ten missed opportunities between January 2020 and August 2021 to act on sources of information held between the CIA and FBI.

- The Commission report highlighted that the only period in which the government seemed to act in concert to deal with terrorism was the last weeks of December 1999 preceding the millennium. Everyone was on edge with the millennium and computer programming glitches (also known as "Y2K") that might obliterate records, shut down power and communication lines or disrupt daily life. This showed that the government could mobilize itself at scale for an alert against terrorism. While one factor was the preexistence of widespread concern about Y2K, another was simply that information was being actively shared.

- Ironically, Y2K would also be the event that launched my career in business continuity, which we shall discuss further under *Chapter 16, Opportunity.*

Lessons we can learn from this

- The case study and events leading up to 9/11 highlight issues that exist across many organizations internally and externally – which can be attributed to ineffective information sharing and overall accountability for taking affirmative action based on the content of that information.

- There is potentially a misconception about who does what within an organization and assumptions that someone, somewhere, must be doing something. With the closer integration between digital technology and operational networks, organizations can no longer work in isolation

- There is often a danger, as we have examined in previous case studies, of downplaying the severity of reports and threats. There is often a disconnect between information that may be known on the ground by workers and what is reported to upper management. Often both are oblivious to the extent of communication and verification that each party believes to have been made to the other. As identified under *Chapter 4, Communication*.

- This highlights broader management issues pertaining to how the top leaders of organizations set priorities and allocate resources. The highest-priority issues might not get the maximum support that they need to be effectively managed and resolved. This can also be indicative of a culture that does not enable constructive challenge to management and the priorities and decisions they must make, often in challenging circumstances.

- The case study also highlights common issues associated with the lack of collective analysis and monitoring from combined threats and correlating this together, not just to look for patterns but also inconsistencies in that data, and the requirement to turn such information into actionable intelligence and '*Knowledge.*'

- As discussed in *Chapter 2, Actions*, people can only make decisions based on information that is available at the time. When data is flawed or missing, or assumptions are made about the credibility and accuracy of the information, you can see how the resulting decision and actions may turn out to be wrong.

- It is, therefore, important that the intended outcome and decisions that management is being asked to make are clearly articulated, as are the consequences if no decision or action is made.

Importance of isomorphic learning

There is a need to consider the principle of isomorphic learning, which can broadly be described as two or more parallel incidents that have different causes but the same outcome. This is an example of why we principally need to plan for the impact of an incident rather than the cause. For example, whether a train driver ignores a red signal or there is an incorrect signal, this could still cause a train to crash and derail.

The issue with such events is that organizations may fail to see the correlation between events.

Similarly, the two events mentioned earlier in the book with regard to the Piper Alpha oil rig disaster in 1988 and the B.P. Deep Water Horizon oil rig in 2010. The causes of both incidents and the events that led up to the incidents are different, but the outcome was the same – multiple explosions and fatalities.

Our ability to understand how and why major incidents occur, and the events leading up to them, can help us systematically reduce the probability of a recurrence.

If we do not acknowledge our failings and wrongdoings, we end up oblivious to the threats on the horizon. We are not prepared.

Applying lessons

After every incident, audit, or test, we need to analyze what worked well and what did not. We learn so much from our failings, and in fact, we learn more than if things went to plan - it raises our awareness, challenges our perception, and increases our *'Knowledge'* and experience. This gives us more confidence in our decision-making.

Every innovation and invention is a variant of what preceded it. We simply learn, improve, and advance each time.

Our past is a good indicator of what is to come, so let us use it to our advantage since we know that history has a habit of repeating itself. This requires a willingness and desire to apply deep learning by looking for patterns of association to break the cycle.

So, if you receive a report with red or high risks, treat it as a blessing and a great opportunity to learn and improve.

Do not just simply file it away with the others.

Conclusion

This chapter asked us to evaluate why we appear to be destined to repeat history and how and why we need to break the cycle. Previous events are a good indicator of what is on the horizon and the opportunities that we have to alter the trajectory by taking deliberate and decisive action to enable positive change.

Reflection

- What is your impression of the case study in terms of how disparate information relating to a viable threat was collected and disseminated?

- What is the organization's overall stance on active learning? When a report is received that highlights negative aspects, is it welcomed as an opportunity to improve or is it buried away?

- Does the organization apply isomorphic learning from events that have occurred to similar organizations in the industry, or are they ignored?

- When faced with evolving threats, does the organization regard investment in resilience as an important business differentiator or a cost center?

Suggested actions

- Document the measures by which the organization will identify investment requirements for enabling effective resilience.

- Ensure that after every test, training, audit, and investigation, there is an opportunity for reflection. This should not only focus on what happened and why but also on how people personally dealt with the incident and what lessons they learned.

- Ensure there is a commitment to turn lessons into opportunities to improve and to promote a deeper commitment to establishing resilience to such events.

In the next chapter, I shall explore the role of the *'Media'* in a crisis and whether you regard them as a friend or foe.

CHAPTER 14
Media

During a major incident, it is surprising how many organizations will try and keep things out of the public domain and will avoid the media at all costs.

As I highlighted in *Chapter 4, Communication*, if the incident is going to warrant concern from your stakeholders, it is best practice to tell them before they tell you. You may also be legally obligated in some jurisdictions to report on specific incidents.

So, let us start with a popular misconception – the media is not your enemy. In fact, find a trusted media outlet, and they can be one of your strongest advocates. Responsible journalists have a similar desire to establish and report on the truth.

Structure

In this chapter, I will discuss the following:

- Reliance on the media in a crisis

- Communicating with the media

- Dealing with censorship

Objectives

The objective of this chapter is to establish the role that the media plays in a crisis and why they need to be treated as a key stakeholder. When ignored, journalists may be forced to go digging for a story and may be more inclined to misinterpret or misreport the facts. It is, therefore, in your interest to ensure that the organization is represented in the right way and that sources are credible. I shall also explore why censorship and banning content only leads people to ask more questions about why.

Reliance on the media in a crisis

We all want to read credible information, so let us make sure we are contributing to it by reducing the instances of creating and sharing misinformation and identifying and ruling out disinformation.

Also, consider that you are reliant on the media and accurate information in an incident, particularly if you are trying to gather information to make decisions. Consider the credibility of the source, and impact if that is wrong, and the consequences. This is one of the reasons why I highlighted the importance of removing assumptions in *Chapter 2, Actions*.

In *Chapter 12, Knowledge*, I shared the importance of understanding the evolving threat of *'information wars,'* with how disinformation can be propagated and amplified by state-sponsored media, and how this can be utilized to influence a politically motivated agenda by targeting diverse groups of the population. This is typically performed over a period or in relation to the *'news of the day'* where people are reacting to a specific topic.

Most successful cyberattacks - whether it is phishing, business email compromise, ransomware, or disinformation, have one thing in common, and that is the power of persuasion and manipulation.

Sensationalist *'clickbait'* headlines, and stories utilized by the media, are another example of how people can be lured into reading or believing specific content.

Arguably, people may assume that if an article is written by a journalist, then that person will have done their research and checked their facts when we know this is not always the case; after all, journalists are also under pressure to report their *'stories'* in a timely manner or be the first to break a news story. Journalists may be able to redact stories, but the doubt is already there.

This is one of the reasons that I highlighted the need to consider the trustworthiness and credibility of sources when it comes to professional and unbiased journalism. Some media outlets can also be politically motivated or be known for publishing satire rather than fact.

Communicating with the media

Remember the facts versus fiction we spoke about in *Chapter 7, Facts*? When dealing with the media, it is important to communicate the facts. Do not leave room for speculation or rumor.

The communication should be *'Believable'* and *'Honest,* and demonstrate true *'Empathy'* for those impacted, and delivered with *'Gravitas.'* The media are well versed at seeing through communications that lack sincerity or conviction, so a pre-prepared statement that is peppered with buzzwords will be obvious to a journalist.

If you speak with confidence and have a willingness and desire to provide factual and timely communications, the media are less likely to report misinformation or go looking for a story.

Do not be aggressive with the media. This could be misconstrued that the organization is trying to hide information, and the media is more likely to want to explore this avenue further by asking more specific lines of questions or by pursuing different lines of inquiry to elicit a response.

In the opening line of this book, I make a clear and deliberate statement that *'the way in which a major change or incident is handled is often more important than the incident itself'* – this is especially relevant when handling the media.

The way in which the media chooses to report a story can have a large bearing on how the organization is perceived by the public and other key stakeholders. Do you want to be shown as a company that is empathetic and caring or one that is the antagonist? This can also be amplified across social media channels, as other media outlets, organizations, and individuals add comments and speculation to what is reported or, conversely, what is not reported.

A few things to consider - '*no comment*' is still a comment. And there is no such thing as off the record. Be careful of being misquoted or words being taken out of context.

Whilst people can naturally be nervous about talking to journalists live on camera. It can also help to ensure that information is reported as is and not taken out of context. To caveat this, those people who are chosen to be spokespersons for the organization need to have received media training and be cognizant of how journalists may try and ask difficult questions in an attempt to stir emotions. This is also why I spoke about the need to identify people with '*Gravitas*' who can respond well under pressure.

Whilst you may identify trained and authorized spokespeople, it is important that everyone in the organization knows what to do if they are asked for information by the media and to be mindful of what they say and to whom. Therefore, ensure that employees remain briefed, which is one of the reasons why we highlight the importance of including your employees as key stakeholders in *Chapter 4, Communication*, and why they can be one of the organization's biggest advocates for reinforcing key messages.

An employee of the company could be construed as a representative, so everyone needs to know how to report a media inquiry, in much the same way as how to report an IT or security incident.

Just like other stakeholders, there should be a commitment to regular and consistent updates from a nominated spokesperson(s) as further information is available. If a rapport has been developed with the media, it is advisable to continue to utilize the same people, to build trust and credibility with the messaging. Conversely, if there are perceptions with a lack of believability or sincerity, it is advisable to consider a change in approach or spokesperson.

Dealing with censorship

It should be noted that in many countries, individuals are protected under laws and regulations pertaining to freedom of expression and freedom of speech. Therefore, you need to be mindful of some legislation when you try and block certain content.

Of course, there will be times when injunctions are raised to prevent the reporting of certain information, but that usually pertains to the protection of victims, where reporting or misreporting could prejudice the outcome of a case or harm the victim.

Banning specific content and people can potentially have the opposite effect, as people may be driven to ask why and seek answers for themselves. Banning content is usually done after the fact, so it has already been disseminated, or screenshots taken by people, which can just be reposted.

This can mean that certain websites and content is driven underground and can deliver a level of notoriety that only seeks to reinforce the content. Such content could include manipulating people to agree or oppose extremist or radicalized views and opinions. This can be indicative of how the people behind the distribution of content can utilize censorship and embargoes to their advantage.

Organizations still need to protect themselves and their brand from defamatory and libelous content, but they should also consider the source and motivation behind such content, as discussed in *Chapter 7, Facts* and the impact of misinformation and disinformation.

Conclusion

In this chapter, I explored why the media is not your enemy in a crisis. In fact, when handled correctly, they can be an excellent resource for amplifying and sharing key messages. Since we all have the desire to access and consume credible and factual information, we need to ensure we are contributing to it. This helps to build trust in the organization through transparency.

Reflection

- What is the organization's overall stance on communicating and liaising with the media? Has this generally been favorable or antagonistic in the past?

- Do you have trusted media outlets and journalists for proactive outreach and promotion of the organization?

- Do you have mechanisms in place to identify when articles or social media posts are published about the organization or key individuals and whether these are factually accurate? What is your stance when looking to correct or dispute such articles or posts?

Suggested actions

- Create a strategy for media liaison and identify how and when news will be published to the press. Establish several trusted news outlets that can be utilized for proactive outreach and engagement.

- Thinking back to the communication strategy in *Chapter 4, Communication*, determine how and when you will communicate with the media and whether you will have a nominated spokesperson(s). Larger organizations may identify several people with different skill sets.

- Determine whether there is a need to engage the support of a public relations person to help liaise with the media in different scenarios. This type of relationship needs to have been established in advance of a specific incident.

- Consider that whilst the media may request interviewing specific people, consider how appropriate that is and whether they have received appropriate training and guidance.

- Ensure that all people in the organization have received training and awareness about what to do if they are approached by the media for comment. Note that this can happen at any time and not just during an incident since any employee can be construed as a representative of the organization.

In the next chapter, I shall explore what happens when you encounter a *'Near-miss'*. Do you simply move on or treat it as an opportunity to learn and improve?

CHAPTER 15
Near Miss

When you have an incident that could have been major but was avoided '*just in time,*' do you perform a full review, or mop your brow, think you were lucky, and move on?

I have been there. Those heart-wrenching moments when you are in full swing and about to pull the trigger to invoke a business continuity or crisis management plan, and then the lights/systems come back online as if by magic!

It is an awkward moment where you wait and watch, monitor for a while, and then go back to normal, safe in the knowledge that all is well.

Apart from this little nagging voice, which says…but '*what if*'?

Structure

In this chapter, I will discuss the following:

- A game of chance

- Incident containment

- What would happen next?

Objectives

The aim of this chapter is to explore why we fail to learn lessons from near misses and how we can turn this into opportunities to improve the overall crisis response. The next time a near miss occurs might just be the catalyst that triggers a more serious event. Expect questions to be asked on why you failed to act when an incident occurred that could have been avoided.

A game of chance

Near misses should be treated like the real thing, must be logged, must be analyzed, and '*Actions*' recorded. It is an opportunity to pose '*Questions*' and consider the '*what if*' in a safe environment, against a range of scenarios, to determine the next steps and preparedness. A slight change in parameters could have had a different outcome - so take the time to explore the possibilities.

Ignoring near-misses breeds complacency, and there can be a tendency for this to be regarded as the norm when in fact, this could be the trigger or catalyst for a more severe incident if left unresolved.

By failing to analyze and deal with near misses, we are simply waiting for the next event.

Do not treat near-misses like a game of chance.

Incident containment

The reason the near miss never escalated beyond a minor incident, or was contained within a sufficient timescale, can also be a testament to the training, awareness, and resilience that has already been instigated by the organization to limit and resolve the impact as efficiently as possible. As we shall discuss in later chapters, not only are these valuable '*Lessons*,' but they provide a great '*Opportunity*' and can also be viewed as a '*Victory*' if correct evasive actions and procedures are followed.

The important lesson is to consider the overall '*Strategy*' and '*Actions*' that were deployed or not deployed, to look for opportunities to improve the process, or to ratify any decisions or actions that may have been taken if the incident had progressed.

What would happen next?

When considering the context of the near-miss and what would have potentially happened if the incident were not resolved or contained, it is necessary to look forward and consider the consequences and impact of those actions that did not take place.

In a controlled environment with relevant parties, allow the incident to play out as part of an exercise to examine the circumstances that enabled the incident to be declared a near miss and what could have happened if the incident progressed beyond the current state. Since the exercise is based on a real incident, it provides credibility to the scenario, and people may be more inclined to '*Investigate*' and examine each stage of the incident. We shall discuss more about tests and exercises in *Chapter 20, Strategy.*

It is worth bearing in mind, however, that some people can be stuck in hindsight without focusing on the lessons learned and looking forward. Once they know more about an event and when they look back with that mindset, emotions of guilt or shame may arise, which is normal. Consider how you can enable people to go backward and take a rational look at what they did and when and whether they would have done the same thing. This emotional disassociation technique helps action owners and decision-makers focus on the lessons learned and overcome the emotion of shame, regret, or guilt – so they can move forward and learn from the experience.

It should also be assumed that unless decisive actions are taken to understand and fix the underlying cause of the near miss, it will more than likely repeat itself. This is why we want to have a critical review and learn from the experience.

Systematically reviewing and analyzing near misses contributes to the overall *'Knowledge'* of the participants and whether they are prepared should a similar incident manifest again.

Conclusion

The saying *'don't look a gift horse in the mouth'* was made for this exact type of scenario. An incident that was contained before it escalated provides a perfect opportunity for analysis, training, and awareness. If you simply move on and do nothing, you have missed a chance to drive effective change or even celebrate a victory.

Reflection

- What is the organization's overall stance on measuring and recording near misses?

- Think back to previous examples of near misses and how these were handled. Are there opportunities to go back and review these to understand the circumstances surrounding them and what actions can be taken as a result?

Suggested actions

- Thinking back to the action plan in *Chapter 2, Action*, ensure there is a mechanism for identifying and reporting on near misses. Determine what actions and decisions need to be taken as a result of the overall incident and crisis management approach.

The next chapter really brings this subject to life as we explore the value of seizing each *'Opportunity'* that comes your way and how you can turn each negative situation into a positive one.

CHAPTER 16
Opportunity

O = OPPORTUNITY

"In the midst of every crisis lies great opportunity."

—*Albert Einstein, German Physicist*

When we only see a crisis as something to be avoided at all costs, we miss the opportunity it represents to make changes. Often the more significant the event, the more impactful and meaningful the change ensues.

Steady incremental steps are good, but what if we took the opportunity to make a positive leap forward for everyone? Not because we must but because we want to.

Structure

In this chapter, I will discuss the following:

- Beyond the comfort zone

- A leap of faith

- Encountering seismic change

- Pivoting into crisis management

- Dare to be bold

- Turning negatives into positives

Objectives

If we accept that we should have an assume compromise and failure mindset and that major incidents will occur, we need to ensure that we seize the opportunities that they represent. The aim of this chapter is, therefore, to recognize those bad things that happen and how we can turn each negative into a positive. There will be times in your professional or personal life when you will have difficult choices to make in terms of the path you take. Will you take the path well-trodden or choose to operate beyond your comfort zone? You may be surprised about the journey ahead.

Beyond the comfort zone

Being pushed beyond your comfort zone can seem frightening, especially if you've also experienced trauma. It is a sign of emotional resilience when you can face your fears and realize you are stronger than you think in the face of adversity.

It requires a mindset shift to make a fundamental cultural change. A willingness and desire to go bigger, bolder, and keep pushing the boundaries.

You would think that after 25 years, I would be a cynic, but the opposite is true. Somewhere along the road, I decided not to let a crisis or adverse events become a wasted opportunity. I have developed an optimism to keep pushing forward.

I want to share a little about how I seized opportunities in my personal life and career and why sometimes you need to believe in yourself and your capabilities.

A leap of faith

As discussed in the next chapter, '*People*', I have always been fascinated with people's welfare, security, and safety. It is one of the key things that drives me, even though I did not understand that from an early age.

I never had a set course about what I wanted to do as a career. There were a few options presented to me at career fairs besides business studies. One of my favorite subjects at school was art – I had the best teacher who would encourage me to use my imagination to its fullest and not be constrained. He would bring out bigger and bigger canvasses for me to paint on. He saw a spark of creativity in me, and I was inspired to want to do something with art – so I looked at becoming a graphic designer.

However, in the early days of college, I was told to draw what I saw – lots of bottles – repeatedly and not use my imagination. It was boring, uninspiring, and dulled my creativity, so I decided to enter the workplace after college.

One of the first roles to pique my interest came in 1996 when I was working in a fraud department for a fleet management company. I would come to learn about the insider threat and what makes good people make bad or hasty decisions. Most of them were opportunists faced with the ability to make some money due to lax processes. Typically, these were ex-employees of an organization who retained fuel cards and would use them to fill up their vehicles. Most of the time, people did not consider it theft or fraud and were mortified that this was the case.

Others knew exactly what they were doing, including, in some instances, the organizations that attempted to defraud the fleet management company to get '*free fuel*' by claiming fuel cards were lost or stolen.

My role was to collate the evidence and perform investigations for potential prosecution. It was fascinating to understand why people did such things – some highlighted it was because they could, and temptation got the better of them rather than malicious intent. Despite how much I enjoyed the role, I was still early in my career.

I joined a water utility company in 1997, working in account management. I did not find it particularly interesting, as it mainly answered customer queries and complaints. I started to look for things to occupy my mind and took every opportunity that came my way. I developed a habit of volunteering for something, despite not knowing what I was putting myself forward for but using it as an opportunity to learn new things. These turned out to be the best decisions I made.

One such opportunity that arose in 1998 was to help compile the annual regulatory compliance report. As a water utility company, strict water quality and pressure requirements exist. One of the requirements was to have a 24-hour emergency call center in case people had no water and to ensure people with special needs were identified to engineers. For example, people who may be on kidney dialysis machines or people who are disabled and unable to go to water bowsers if there is a disruption. I became highly interested in how this information was collated, managed, and reported.

At the start of 1999, another opportunity arose, with the chance to work on a particular IT program – that turned out to be the *millennium bug or Y2K*, as it was more commonly known. The theory was that many computers and servers would not be able to cope as the world entered a new millennium, as internal clocks would revert to their default setting of 01/01/2000, potentially causing multiple system failures across the globe. Many organizations could not take the risk of doing nothing, so they embarked on considerable projects to reprogram the internal clocks of all servers and computers.

My role was to consider all the tests needed at midnight to check that the systems were working correctly. My mind was drawn to the project I had volunteered for the year before, about maintaining an emergency call center. My mind was racing with 'Questions' – what if the systems fail? *What if the call center fails? What if people cannot contact us? What if the water pressure fails? What if people do not have water? What if these are people with special needs?*

I had no idea that these questions were all related to business continuity. In fact, I did not even know this was a subject. It felt like common sense, yet there were not enough satisfactory answers to those questions coming forward. So, I set about a plan – to protect the call center.

For the first time since I left school, my creativity was flowing. I could use my imagination to consider the realm of possibilities and the priority actions required to ensure that the call center could revert to manual processes if needed.

Several projects were instigated to split incoming telephony lines between two service providers, to move the call center agents to an area of the building covered by a generator, to ensure people could get to work if public transport failed, to ensure calls could be taken manually and communicated to engineers in the field. Engineering depots were primed with manual lists of special needs customers with bottled water if needed.

I was in my element. This felt like I was doing something important; it was all about protecting people and those most in need in an emergency.

Many organizations across the globe waited in earnest for the stroke of midnight, and for many, it passed without a hitch. This made the media and others question whether Y2K had been overstated as an issue and was a complete waste of money. Conspiracy theorists would even say that this was the work of technology companies to get people to purchase more equipment.

There was another train of thought that minimal impact happened because of the volume of focus and activity to deliver change and the extent of the planning performed. Cast your mind back to the case study in *Chapter 13, Lessons*, where I discussed 9/11 and the comment made in the Commission Report that the only time when the U.S. government was acting in concert to prepare for terrorism was in the run-up to Y2K, and how people were working to a common goal, by actively sharing information. I really believe this is an important factor when determining the value of proactive contingency planning.

I can at least categorically state that working on the Y2K program launched my career. Over the next 20+ years, I would grow and extend my knowledge, pivoting across business continuity, disaster recovery, crisis management, cybersecurity, and data protection, for several major global organizations.

Not only were there significant events that would change my career trajectory in substantial ways, but these would cause widespread, systematic changes on a large scale across many organizations.

Encountering seismic change

The first seismic change that I experienced was the one that launched my career – the millennium bug. Many IT and resilience professionals have said the same thing over the years. Unlike many other major incidents, this was a known global event and one date that was never going to move – you were either prepared or not at the stroke of midnight. It is estimated that the global costs of planning for an event of this magnitude, including replacing hardware, upgrading software, and resources, amounted to over $300 billion[1].

The following seismic change was, in fact, the 9/11 terrorist attack in 2001, just over one year later. As discussed in case study 3, this was the most significant terrorist attack in U.S. history. Not only did this lead to substantial changes in aviation regulations, but it made many organizations re-evaluate their '*Strategy*' and plans.

At the time, I had just started working for a financial services company. I had moved into disaster recovery, responsible for testing the IT recovery plans. This involved hundreds of backup tapes, with recovery times averaging 48-72 hours. When conjuring up scenarios for events that could feasibly take out an entire Center

---

1   Nir Oren, Real Clear Science, The Millenium Bug was not a Hoax, 1st January, 2020: https://www.realclearscience.com/articles/2020/01/01/the_millennium_bug_was_not_a_hoax_111238.html (retrieved: 26th July 2022)

– it was a plane landing on a building – I did not ever think that this would become a reality.

The shock that rippled from this event would be an acknowledgment for many organizations that they held critical services, data, and people all in one location. A major event, such as 9/11, could destroy everything. This caused many organizations to move data from server rooms into purpose-built remote Data Centers to reduce the impact and to decentralize many operational services to increase resilience.

Many organizations would also consider the need for dual Data Centers with data replication between the two. The issue was compounded by the fact that to have synchronous replication, Data Centers had to be less than 30km from each other and in metropolitan areas. Network costs were incredibly expensive, so this was not a strategy many organizations could not afford, and many were forced to accept the risk.

The next memorable date would come on 7th July 2005 – the day of the *7/7 London bombings* – it would also be my very first day in my new role as a business continuity consultant for a Big 4 professional services firm.

Since 9/11, many organizations have invested heavily in business continuity and disaster recovery. Resources were also at a premium, so I was excited about the opportunity to be able to provide consulting and advisory services to a range of different customers.

For my induction into the organization, I had been invited to join a conference in Amsterdam, Netherlands. Halfway through the morning, the conference organizers announced that there had been a coordinated terrorist attack across London – this was the worst terrorist attack on British soil and just 4 years after 9/11.

Three bombs exploded simultaneously by suicide bombers carrying rug sacks at 08:50, destroying sections of three different London Underground trains. An hour later, at 09:50, there was an explosion on the top level of a double-decker bus caused by a similar device to the ones used underground.

The explosions left fifty-two people dead and over seven hundred injured. Chaos erupted across the capital as London's transport and mobile networks were shut down, fearing more to come.

As the news broke about the bombings, many people at the conference in Amsterdam began to panic, wanting to frantically call colleagues, friends, and family in London to confirm they were safe. However, due to the closure of mobile networks, it was almost impossible to make contact. The conference was closed, and TV screens were brought out so that people could get updates on what was happening in fear of more attacks. The only thing I knew to do was to hold the hand of the woman next to me in silence.

Further coordinated attacks were attempted and thwarted by intelligence agencies on 21 July 2005.

The suicide bombings were confirmed as British citizens with links to Islamic extremists, and the subsequent public inquiry[2] would highlight how quickly the bombers had been radicalized. In much the same way as in the aftermath of 9/11, many questions were raised about previous warnings and the level of intelligence known at the time, which would be indicative of a credible threat. The inquiry would again point to a lack of shared information and profiling of which people could be susceptible to extremist views. In addition, how transport networks presented an attractive target for terrorists.

The public would again live in trepidation and fear for what may be on the horizon.

Pivoting into crisis management

For the firm I had just joined, multiple customers started to request coordinated and large-scale exercises to validate their strategy and response. My focus would pivot from business continuity and disaster recovery into crisis management and consider and plan for the Board level response to mitigate and manage significant events. A few months after 7/7, I enrolled at the Center for Disaster and Emergency Management at Coventry University to enable me to gain deeper learning of academic research into how and why such events occur and what we can learn from them.

In 2007, I joined a global IT service provider and entered the world of cybersecurity. Planning for major incidents and outages had moved from not just considering the physical threats but the impact of digital threats as social media was taking off in a big way. Many organizations were investing in e-Commerce, which created an internet boom. Threats were evolving on a scale.

In 2008, the world experienced a global financial crisis[3] due to excessive risk-taking and lending by several large financial institutions, which led to the collapse and bankruptcy of Lehman Brothers. A firm once thought too big to fail. Governments attempted to bail out many institutions, but they could not stop *'The Great Recession'*, which was about to hit the world. As a result, many people lost their livelihoods and homes, causing considerable distrust in financial services and the government. Many regulation changes and responsible lending ensued.

---

2 Intelligence and Security Committee, Report into the London Terrorist Attacks on 7 July 2005, May 2006: https://assets.publishing.service.gov.uk/government/uploads/system/uploads/attachment_data/file/224690/isc_terrorist_attacks_7july_report.pdf (retrieved 26 July 2022)

3 2008-2009 Global Financial Crisis, The Great Recession, Corporate Financial Institute, 6 May 2022: https://corporatefinanceinstitute.com/resources/knowledge/finance/2008-2009-global-financial-crisis/ (retrieved 26 July 2022)

At a point where many people had already suffered through several significant events, this was a tipping point for many who now found themselves in extreme poverty.

2009 would also become *'my year of crisis'*. It made me appreciate and understand the importance of emotional resilience. I will describe why this year was so eventful, and how this started to take its toll on me in *Chapter 24, Wellbeing*.

In just 10 years since the start of the millennium, we have seen how several events have caused seismic changes. As the world became more digitally connected and dependent on each other, the impact of events created a ripple effect across the supply chain.

What sets organizations apart is how you show up when things are going wrong and which organizations are willing to disrupt themselves.

Fast forward another 10 years to May 2019, and it would lead me to author an article on LinkedIn, where I explored the future of business continuity, how this would evolve over the next 5 years, and how we can build *'Resilience'* in the face of adversity.

It led me to conclude that traditional risk functions, such as business continuity, disaster recovery, cybersecurity, physical security, and health & safety, must be complementary and advanced in parallel.

Within these capabilities are great problem solvers, analytical thinkers, and strategists, often with in-depth *'Knowledge'* and understanding of the business, the sector they operate in, and the threat landscape. However, they must also be adaptive and reactive to change. Not every change is negative, and some can deliver positive outcomes.

Rather than turning away from the biggest threats to cause a disruption, they should be tackled head-on. This entails continuously building and stress-testing the response to build confidence in the capability that engenders trust in the brand.

Ironically, we would see the start of the COVID19 global pandemic a few months later. In addition, it would be one of the most significant scale events to deliver massive levels of positive change. Many organizations went from a place of uncertainty and doubt at the outset of the pandemic to operating in ways that may have seemed incomprehensible just a few years ago.

Dare to be bold

In April 2020, I became the Chief Security Advisor at one of the most prominent technology organizations on the planet – Microsoft - where I was going to be able to deliver my most significant impact to date. It benefited me from working alongside many organizations across multiple sectors, and countries as the challenges and resolutions to those changes revealed themselves. The need for sharing and collaboration, and the value this has on influencing strategic decisions and evolving business models, has never been greater.

I joined Microsoft as multiple organizations contended with the first of many waves of lockdown. There was a rush to ensure services remained available and accessible. Despite the closure of many physical locations, digital services had to stay open as demand soared.

As the weeks turned into months and the first anniversary passed, apprehension eased, and stories of defiance started to appear. The rhetoric of *"we can't do this"* gave way to *"we must do this."* The risk-averse became risk-tolerant.

If there is one thing we know about *'People'* — when faced with major global events and extreme adversity, we can bounce back stronger and rebuild. To do so requires us to innovate continuously.

So, as we come out the other side of an event that has rocked the world, we all have a vast opportunity to dare to be bold and dare to be different.

Turning negatives into positives

Not to get too scientific, but in the world of electrons, a positive charge can be derived from a negative. It is the positive charge that gives us higher potential and power. Sometimes you need a negative to enable a flow to the positive.

Metaphorically speaking, the more positive charge we can generate from negative experiences, the more significant the impact we can have. It is what ultimately led me to author this book and share these experiences.

Unless such tragic events are utilized to shine a light on and drive positive change, we will be destined to have more wasted opportunities.

When faced with major incidents, whether personal or professional, I implore people to consider how they can turn a negative into a positive and shift mindsets as a result – it starts and ends with *'People,'* which we shall explore next.

Conclusion

In this chapter, I have discussed the importance of not dwelling on the negative but seizing each opportunity that arises. Whilst major incidents and events will continue to occur, and if we are to break the cycle, we need to be bold. When we take the time for reflection and choose to make a positive impact and change, it can give people hope for what is on the horizon and that they can weather whatever storms may be coming their way. This is a core component of *'Resilience'* when we are not afraid to shy away from what lies ahead.

Reflections

- A question I asked you at the outset of the book was, *what motivates you?* Have you shared this with anyone? Perhaps it's time for you to let the world know!

- Thinking back to where you delivered positive change, either in a work or personal environment. How did this make you feel? How did it make the people around you feel? Have you identified the opportunities that enable you to replicate this?

- Now bringing this back to your organization, what is the overall approach to managing change –this could be forced upon the organization due to external influences, or the organization itself could generate this. Perhaps the organization is moving into new markets, launching new products and services, upsizing, or downsizing. The point is that how the organization manages and communicates the change plays a significant part in how people will react and adapt to it. If the difference is viewed negatively by employees or other interested parties, what can you do to turn the negativity into a positive one? How can you make this a positive experience?

Suggested actions

- Nobody likes to be in a major incident or crisis, it can be incredibly stressful, and it will undoubtedly unearth many issues and areas of improvement. Thinking back to *Chapter 13, Lessons,* and ensuring there is a commitment to turn lessons into opportunities – write actions in a way that helps people understand the value and the rationale for the action and the difference it will make.

In the next chapter, I will discuss the reason why '*People*' are the most important factor and priority in any incident or crisis.

CHAPTER 17
People

P = PEOPLE

"There can be no greater gift than that of giving one's time and energy to help others without expecting anything in return."

—*Nelson Mandela, South African President, and Activist*

Please repeat this little mantra after me: *'People First Always'* – it is that simple!

I could end the chapter there, and I hope you will agree with this statement, but I also wanted to share some personal insights relating to my *'Why.'*

Structure

In this chapter, I will discuss the following-

- Nothing is more important than people

- People over profit

- The unpredictability of people

Objectives

The aim of this chapter is to highlight why assessing the impact on people is your number one priority during any major incident or crisis – whether directly or indirectly. People are inherently complex, and their actions may sometimes appear to be unpredictable and even irrational, so a key objective is for us to understand this, so we can consider the most appropriate response. I also want to share some reflections from my own childhood and why having a human-centric approach to resilience is so important.

Nothing is more important than people.

I would hope that putting people first, ahead of every other decision, would be an obvious statement. Still, I wanted to highlight why my interest and fascination with all aspects of people's physical and psychological safety and wellbeing started well before forming a large part of my career and why this was instilled into me at a young age.

My father worked as a Sergeant in the Royal Air Force in the military hospitals, where he was a psychiatric nurse.

On 2 April 1982, Argentina invaded the Falkland Islands, a British independent territory, following a dispute over sovereignty. What ensued was a 10-week conflict between Argentina and the UK. This would be the first time since World War II in which all branches of the British armed forces were deployed simultaneously. During the conflict, 255 British military personnel, 3 Islanders, and 648 Argentinian military personnel died.

Many who returned from the conflict started to experience the effects of *Post-Traumatic Stress Disorder (PTSD)*. Although the impact of PTSD on military personnel was widely known, it had only been formally diagnosed as a medical condition in 1980 by the *American Psychiatric Association*. It was still in its infancy, and some considered it a controversial subject. The understanding and treatment for PTSD will continue to evolve over the coming years.

I was six years old and beginning to appreciate what was happening worldwide during the Falklands War. I would never really understand what was going on in the minds of military personnel who had suffered significant physical and emotional trauma. Still, I became aware of the need for empathy and care for those that needed it most. I would remember the peace of the military hospitals where my father was stationed and those who required treatment, convalescence, and time. We shall talk more about emotional resilience and dealing with trauma in *Chapter 23, Wellbeing*.

Also, in the 1980s, the *Irish Republican Army (IRA)* increased their attacks on British targets, service personnel, and their families. The anticipation and planning for car bombs and shootings stepped up. At the time, my family was stationed at the Joint Head Quarters for British Forces and elements of NATO in Rheindahlen, Germany. I became acutely aware each time the threats escalated, as there would be an increase in armed guards and patrols at the military base, and even school buses were checked for devices. There was often fear when tensions escalated, but I somehow felt safe, knowing that people had been trained to care for us and would keep us safe from harm.

I do not know if I was always destined to have a career centered on the security and welfare of people or if it just turned out that way, but I seized the opportunities as they arose, with a desire to keep learning.

We must consider that people's experiences and how they shape their life will be influenced from an early age. If we want to change mindsets and perceptions, this needs to start way before people enter the workplace, when they first begin understanding the world they live in and how it influences their actions and decisions, whether or not they realize it.

People will remember how you made them feel, positively or negatively, more than the words you said. We also discussed how you could engender trust at all levels during *Chapter 6, Empathy*.

People over profit

When I state that people should come before profit, I am sure you will think this is an obvious statement. However, I have lost count of how many times I have seen people's safety, security, and wellbeing as no. 3-4 on an incident response plan list, even coming lower than financial or technological impact.

Irrespective of the type of incident, your assessment of the impact on people - whether directly or indirectly - should always be your top priority.

As we explored during *Chapter 5, Diligence*, a decision to act or not act, based predominantly on financial metrics and not the safety and welfare of people, will not end favorably. In the case of Ford and Bridgestone, the organization's economic impact was much higher than if it had chosen to act sooner.

After all, everything affects people in one way or another, especially when you consider all those involved in the management and operation of the incident and those that any downstream impact may impact because of loss of service. We must think about what we are trying to protect and why.

If there is a criminal element to the incident, remember who the victims are and what support they may need.

A human-centric mindset is essential when considering any decision and action, and people must be front and center of that to enable the best outcome for all.

The unpredictability of people

People are complex social beings and a construct of their environment, culture, and belief systems. As I explore in this book, many factors are at play when understanding why people act as they do.

People are not inherently good or bad, even if their actions may appear that way. Even those who have committed heinous crimes against others are still capable of having loving and functional relationships.

Some may be driven by desperation, fear, stress, or greed. Decisions that seem perfectly rational for some will be irrational for others. External forces can influence and manipulate this, whether they are aware of it or not.

The point is that we cannot predict what people will do in any given situation.

As much as we want to have good intent within our organization and put people front and center of our decisions, some also wish to create as much harm and disruption as possible.

The case studies show that some of these acts require massive planning, resources, determination, and persistence. Therefore, we should not underestimate the will and motivation of people who wish to inflict harm, whether directly through acts of violence, such as terrorist attacks, or indirectly, such as cyberattacks and disinformation campaigns.

Conversely, we should not underestimate the will and motivation required to prevent or limit such acts' impact and bring such perpetrators to justice.

As I stated in the *Introduction*, our role as incident and crisis responders is to expect the unexpected, and the unpredictability of people is a key principle that we have covered in many examples.

As I shall discuss further in *Chapter 19, Resilience* and *Chapter 20, Strategy,* our level of planning and preparedness must be commensurate with the internal and external risks and threats the organization faces. Still, you also cannot plan for every conceivable underlying cause of an incident.

Conclusion

In this chapter, I have discussed why there is nothing more important than people. Considering how to protect the needs and welfare of people is central to the overall strategy for resilience. It is also a key factor when establishing how the organization's culture can help or hinder the effectiveness of the strategy.

Reflection

- Consider the organization's overall stance on incidents and crisis management. What are the thresholds and criteria for declaring a major incident or crisis? Where do people appear on the list of priorities? Are these featured at the top?

Suggested actions

- Thinking back to the action plan in *Chapter 2, Action* and *Chapter 4, Communication 4,* ensure that every action and communication is prioritized on assessing and maintaining health, safety, security, and welfare of people first. This includes those directly involved in the management of the incident.

- Ensure that each action and consequence is assessed on how it may benefit or impact people.

- Thinking back to *Chapter 14, 'Media',* pre-empt what journalists may want to know about how the incident affects people. Be clear at the outset of your statements about what you are doing to support those people impacted either directly or indirectly. Remember what I discussed on demonstrating *'Empathy'.*

In the next chapter, I shall explore the subject of *'Questions'* – which ones will be key to answering before, during, and after a crisis.

CHAPTER 18
Questions

I do not mind admitting I am someone who likes to ask lots of questions. Telling me, '*This is how it's always been,*' is guaranteed to make me want to ask even more questions! I am a bonafide challenger of the status quo!

Call it a natural curiosity and a genuine desire to understand more, but those questions are essential for education and obtaining and verifying '*Knowledge.*' It is also part of our role as incident and crisis responders to find the underlying cause of what is happening, reduce the unknowns, and close the gaps.

There are no genuinely no stupid questions because others are probably thinking them too.

Structure

In this chapter, I will discuss the following:

- Questions to ask pre-incident

- Questions to ask during an incident

- Questions to ask post-incident

Objectives

This chapter explores why it's a good idea to ask lots of questions before, during, and after an incident. Simply accepting things as they are does little to improve the situation. It is good practice to enable people to consider whether the expected '*Actions*' are still appropriate to the scenario and whether they will still have the intended outcomes. It is also good practice to encourage different opinions and expertise. Blindly following a rigid plan may lead to unintended consequences.

Questions to ask pre-incident

Two proactive questions that have come to be so important when considering a range of scenarios for what could go wrong in advance of any incident are:

- What if?

- So what?

Pretty easy to remember.

The '*what if*' is predicated on assuming failure or compromise across every element of the organization. This enables you to identify potential gaps and vulnerabilities that could be exploited deliberately or accidentally.

The '*so what*' is predicated on the impact if such things come to fruition. The higher the impact, enables us to identify and prioritize the actions needed to close the vulnerabilities.

An assume compromise and failure mindset also changes our measurement of risk from a position of something that '*may*' happen to it '*will*' happen if left untreated.

Sometimes organizations can focus too much on the probability and inadvertently ignore those threats that they deem a negligible risk or implausible, even though the impact is substantial.

Therefore, the impact must trump probability every time because, as we have seen in the chosen case studies, although events may be rare, their impact is of such a magnitude that they cannot be ignored or downplayed. The core focus, therefore, rests on the '*severe but plausible*' – use your imagination and creativity to consider the scenarios, as even the weird and wonderful have an ounce of truth behind them. We shall discuss this further in *Chapter 19, Resilience*, and *Chapter 20, Strategy*.

Questions to ask during an incident

As discussed in previous chapters, events can evolve rapidly amid a significant incident or crisis, and conflicting information can often occur.

We must ask ourselves whether we are being logical and systematic in our actions, communication, and decision-making or whether we're potentially making irrational decisions due to pressure from stakeholders and other interested parties. External influences can also drive you towards a specific outcome, whether intended or not.

I have identified that things can quickly go off-piste, requiring you to consider an alternative course of action.

Rather than pressing ahead, it is necessary to take a pause and ask two key questions:

- Are we on track?

- What needs to change?

- What help do you need?

Just taking a short break can help people consider the actions taken or about to be taken, whether this aligns with the overarching organizational strategy and vision, and whether it will have the intended outcomes.

It is essential also to ensure that people are not just rigidly following a plan, and preset actions, if these no longer serve a purpose.

This can also be a great opportunity for people to reflect on their own needs, as well as the needs of others, including identifying what help may be required, either internally or externally. Think of this as an opportunity to recalibrate what has happened so far and what will happen next.

Note that these are open questions. Asking someone, *"Do you need help?"* is more likely to elicit a *"No"* response. Please do not put the onus on the person to feel like they need to ask for help, but instead, collectively determine what needs to happen as a team to contain and resolve the incident.

As we shall discuss in *Chapter 23, Wellbeing,* sometimes the onus will be on you, as the incident and crisis manager, to identify when people need to stop. Consider that the help can come from inside or outside the organization to provide specialist and independent expertise that can also guide further actions and responses.

Questions to ask post incident

Two reactive questions that have come to be so important when considering what went wrong after an incident are:

- How?
- Why?

Again, these are easy questions to remember.

The *'How'* is predicated on understanding the detailed timeline of what happened and when. There is a need to collate information on the *'Actions'* taken and consider all the *'Facts'* as part of an *'Investigation.'*

The *'Why'* is all predicated on what caused the event to occur in the first place. This is about understanding the root cause, as we discuss in *Chapters 25* and *26,* on determining your *'X'* and *'Y.'*

This enables us to learn *'Lessons,'* increase our *'Knowledge'* and identify *'Opportunities'* to deliver effective and proactive change.

This highlights how so many aspects of the crisis response are interconnected. In some respects, this entails us going full circle to question some of our earlier assumptions, armed with the information we have now gained, so we can continuously ratify our response.

Conclusion

In this chapter, we have explored where it is good practice to consider the type of questions that should be asked before, during, and after an incident. As we have discussed throughout the book, taking time to reflect and question whether the plan is still valid enables people to gather their thoughts and consider the decisions and actions required as the situation evolves. People should be encouraged to ask questions and check the validity of the plan and their own understanding of the situation.

Reflection

- Consider the culture within your organization and whether it promotes an open forum for people to raise questions and provide feedback. Does it enable people to challenge current processes and identify areas for improvement?

- Do you have an inquisitive mind when presenting or relying on information? Are you actively challenging and reaffirming the accuracy and source of information rather than taking it at face value?

Suggested actions

- Ensure opportunities are provided to raise open and closed questions before, during, and after a major incident. Determine whether the answers to the questions materially change the proposed actions or plan and why. These need to be documented and communicated to relevant interested parties.

In the next chapter, we shall have a deeper dive into the overall subject of *'Resilience'*, and why this is our ultimate objective

CHAPTER 19
Resilience

When the sum of all the interconnected parts comes together and works in unison, you have resilience. The capacity to bounce back, or jump forward in the face of adversity, requires flexibility, adaptability, and agility. It is not about avoiding major incidents but tackling them head-on with confidence and competence.

That ecosystem of connected parts extends beyond our boundary, and we need to consider the upstream and downstream impact and where we need to bolster our capacity and performance.

Many things are outside our immediate control, but that does not mean we cannot be prepared for them. This requires diligence, a lesson in hindsight to learn from the past, and a lesson in foresight to understand and predict what is on the horizon and beyond.

Structure

In this chapter, I will be discussing the following-

- Future-proofing resilience

- Embracing a culture of resilience and security

- Demonstrating organizational resilience

- Strengthening the resilience of others

Objectives

In this chapter, I shall explore what it really means to be resilient and what, ultimately, we are striving for. The state of resilience is constantly evolving and flexing to the world around us. It is, therefore, imperative that, as an organization, we understand our role in the overall ecosystem and how we can enable a level of resilience and stability for all. Our objective is to support the business's ability to make strategic decisions now and into the future that provides confidence under changing conditions.

Future-proofing resilience

We have established that we should expect the unexpected, and the journey ahead is not straightforward. At each fork in the road, you have choices, and each one has consequences. Considering how each decision and action affects what is to come is imperative.

If we went through life without obstacles, we would not know our strengths and capability. We would not advance our '*Knowledge*' and be willing to accept more risk.

Suppose we consider that economic, environmental, geopolitical, societal, or technological threats will continue to evolve globally. We should '*expect the unexpected*' and that '*anything is plausible*,' we need to consider how we navigate and manage the changing landscape.

This requires resilience in the face of adversity. Resilience is about not being afraid to take a leap, not being afraid to fail and bounce back and repeat. A resilient organization provides longevity, stability, and viability and engenders trust. These organizations see opportunities where others only see risk.

Enabling resilience and seizing opportunities requires multiple '*Strategies*,' not just one. The ability to scan the horizon and gather numerous sources of information is vital, as is the ability to pivot and change trajectory, potentially in multiple directions. Organizations require a microscope to understand the here and now and a telescope to pre-empt and decipher the future. This needs to be controlled, enabling the organization to carefully consider each outcome rather than a misguided reaction to a sudden change or significant incident.

It is not enough for an organization to be resilient while others fail. The resilience of an organization must also consider the resilience of the communities it serves and have a deep appreciation of the complexities of the supply chain.

To be most effective, organizations need to work in partnership based on shared values and vision. This should be based on trust and transparency with the agility to react to major incidents and changes in market conditions as quickly and efficiently as possible, utilizing shared risk for mutual benefit. The ability to share resources and information will be vital and enable each organization to be less vulnerable to disruption.

Embracing a culture of resilience and security

Threats to the resilience of an organization can be caused by a myriad of factors, whether internal or external, malicious or accidental. Often in the case of a malicious attack, criminals will use a multitude of ways to gain access to or infiltrate the organization. This can include bypassing technology and going straight to the source: the people. Organizations need to empower and enable people to become the strongest link so that they can become resilient themselves.

Organizations must consider the wider economic, environmental, and societal risks and opportunities as part of a long-term adaptive strategy. This requires a commitment to providing a positive social impact for current and future generations to enable prosperity.

Having come through a global pandemic, many organizations will state they have demonstrated their resilience, but the truth is that this requires consistency and persistence. All the other threats that existed previously have not gone away. It is just that the world has changed and will continue to evolve, albeit at a rate we may not have envisaged before, as more organizations have a willingness and desire to take more risks.

Demonstrating organizational resilience

I mentioned how I worked for an IT Service Provider for over 12 years. That organization was *Fujitsu*, a Japanese company employing over 100,000 people worldwide.

I want to share a story of resilience in action and how planning large-scale events can pay dividends when faced with a major event.

Let us first consider the geography of Japan, which comprises 6,852 islands stretching over 1,900 miles. Much of the terrain is rugged and mountainous and is restricted for habitation. Thus, the habitable zones, mainly in the coastal areas, have very high population densities.

Japan is substantially prone to earthquakes, tsunamis, and volcanic eruptions because of its location along the Pacific Ring of Fire. Japan has 111 active volcanoes. Destructive earthquakes, often resulting in tsunamis, occur several times each century. The most devasting was the 1923 Tokyo earthquake which killed over 140,000 people.

Many buildings in high-populous areas such as Tokyo, home to c.14 million people, are built to withstand earthquake tremors.

Establishing a level of preparedness

With the high risk and probability of volcano eruptions and earthquakes, Fujitsu had undertaken to prepare for such events by running annual '*Disaster Preparedness*' days. These tend to be large-scale exercises that require months of planning. Such exercises may mimic and simulate the loss and recovery of an entire Data Center or essential building, for example. These had been performed over a period of years.

This level of pre-planning would be tested for real on 11th March 2011, when a powerful magnitude-9.0 earthquake struck the northeastern coast of Japan[1]. The sudden horizontal and vertical thrusting of the Pacific Plate spawned a series of

---

1 John Rafferty, Britanica, Japan earthquake and tsunami of 2011, https://www.britannica.com/event/Japan-earthquake-and-tsunami-of-2011/Relief-and-rebuilding-efforts, (retrieved 12 August 2022)

highly destructive tsunami waves. Within two weeks of the disaster, the Japanese government's official count of deaths had exceeded 10,000 people. The earthquake and tsunami constituted one of the deadliest natural disasters in Japanese history.

The earthquake and tsunami caused significant damage to Japan's infrastructure and affected communities as multiple buildings were destroyed, and many organizations and homes lost power and water for significant periods. What ensued was a huge clean-up operation and a commitment to rebuild. Many organizations had lost their buildings or had no technology or communications.

A commitment to rebuild

The Fujitsu Group was committed[2] to restoring damaged IT systems in the regions with the highest priority on lifeline systems such as power, water, gas, hospitals, and police and fire departments.

In the 2011 Annual Report[3], Fujitsu highlighted a loss of 11.6 billion yen (c.$80 million) to cover costs to restore damaged assets and inventory loss. Despite this, Fujitsu also highlighted the lengths they had gone to support disaster relief efforts. This included:

- Support team dispatched to assist customers centered on local governments, hospitals, and financial institutions

- A range of cloud services provided free of charge for three months to companies and local governments involved in recovery efforts

- Emergency supplies were sent to disaster areas, including compact hybrid power-generating units

- Computers and support for internet access to evacuation centers

- PCs are provided free of charge for Nonprofit Organizations (NPOs) supporting relief efforts

---

2 Fujitsu statement on earthquake in Japan, 15th March 2011, https://www.fujitsu.com/sg/about/resources/news/press-releases/2011/Fujitsu-statement-on-earthquake-in-Japan.html (retrieved 17 Augst 2022)

3 Fujitsu Annual Report 2011, Extract, Fujitsu Group's Response to the Great East Japan Earthquake, 15th July 2011, https://www.fujitsu.com/global/documents/about/ir/library/annual-rep/2011/09.pdf (retrieved 17th August 2022)

Evolving the disaster response

In 2012, Fujitsu announced[4] how the planning for the next set of Disaster Days would include visiting c.5,000 customers to explain the Fujitsu Group's support activities and organizational structure in the event of a disaster.

In addition, the Disaster Day preparation would include a core customer to simulate another large-scale earthquake to evacuate all employees at once from within plants affected by a disaster in real time. At the same time, designated staff members would gather in a predetermined disaster response headquarters installed within the facility.

Fujitsu has continued to review and improve its disaster preparedness and resilience year-on-year, including customers and partners, to determine the response to large-scale events to demonstrate resilience and sustainability.

Strengthening the resilience of others

There is significant value in looking beyond the organization's boundaries by proactively increasing the supply chain's resilience and those providing essential services. In *Chapter 22, 'Underdog'* we discuss the perils and danger of ignoring the underdog, and the misconception when you assume you are too big to fail.

A fundamental part of this book is focused on what to do when you have a major incident. We have identified the issues that occur when things get ignored, not taking opportunities, and not learning lessons all contribute to making us less prepared or resilient.

Conversely, by heeding the lessons and taking proactive action that decisively acts to make the organization more resilient, we can collectively deliver seismic change that benefits everyone, no matter where they reside.

Conclusion

In this chapter, we have discussed what it means to be resilient. We have established that being resilient whilst others are failing does little to help the overall ecosystem. We have explored an example of resilience in action and how organizations can look beyond the boundaries of their own organization to establish how they can enable others to be resilient too. We have further discussed how our objective is not to go through life trying to avoid major incidents but to accept that there are a number of threats that we need to anticipate and plan for.

---

4 Fujitsu, Fujitsu Implements Joint Disaster Response Drills Throughout Japan, 30th August 2012, https://www.fujitsu.com/global/about/resources/news/press-releases/2012/0830-01.html (retrieved 17th August 2022)

Reflection

- How resilient are you today? That may sound like a loaded question, and I ask it deliberately because how do you know? What are you measuring this against? Perhaps your organization has already encountered major events, or you are in the midst of one. How is the organization coping right now?

- If your organization was to directly encounter any of the case studies or examples that I discussed in this book, how prepared would you be? What level of resilience could you demonstrate, and what is missing?

Suggested actions

- Determine the benchmark by which you will measure resilience. Where are you today, and where do you want to be? How long is it going to take to get there?

- Document the roadmap and investment required to achieve the desired state of resilience and what needs to change. As we discussed in *Chapter 16, Opportunity*, this should be focused on how you will deliver positive change and business enablement that provides confidence to interested parties on how the organization will manage adversity. As I highlighted from the outset, this also needs to be grounded on your *'Why'* – what is driving the need for change? Do not be afraid to ask or answer those difficult *'Questions.'* I spoke about this in the previous chapter.

- Like the overall incident and crisis management strategy and plan, ensure that the roadmap is designed to pivot and adapt to the economic, environmental, geopolitical landscape and other vital threats. While it is great to have a 3–5-year strategy and outlook, a lot can happen in that time. A roadmap or plan that is too rigid and does not adapt may not yield the required results.

The next chapter is intrinsically linked to this one, as your overall approach to resilience hinges on your *'Strategy'*, which is what we shall explore next.

CHAPTER 20
Strategy

S = STRATEGY

"I am prepared for the worst but hope for the best."

—*Benjamin Disraeli, Former U.K. Prime Minister*

Imagine if the worst-case scenario is on your doorstep. Have you got a strategy? Have you told people what it is? Have you documented it and practiced what you will do?

Have you got a Plan B, C, or D, for when things go wrong?

Can you stop, pivot, and change directions?

Having a strategy and plan for when things go wrong is good, but it cannot be rigid. You must constantly evaluate whether your '*Actions*' are valid and achieve the desired outcome.

You cannot plan for every conceivable scenario, but there are certainly some things you should be clear on in terms of key decisions and what your objective is during a crisis.

Structure

In this chapter, I shall discuss the following:

- Strategy and culture
- Developing scenarios
- Exercising the crisis response

Objectives

The aim of this chapter is to highlight the key scenarios that should be considered as part of the overall crisis response and resilience strategy. We shall consider the principle of cause versus effect when it comes to effective planning and testing of the response.

Strategy and culture

The quote '*culture eats strategy for breakfast*' is attributed to Peter Drucker, the management and education scholar. This means that no matter how good your strategy is, its efficacy will be held back if the people implementing it are not on board or do not feel valued.

Remember what we said about making '*People*' front and center to every decision, that you are '*Believable*,' have conviction, and can lead the organization through a crisis by demonstrating '*Gravitas*' and '*Honesty*.'

Your people are your biggest allies, look after them, and they will look after you.

Developing scenarios

Having worked in business continuity and crisis management for many years, I have found that many organizations rarely go anywhere near their worst-case scenario; some have not even articulated what that may be. If we needed further evidence of the impact that such events can cause, we only need to refer to the case studies selected for this book.

Sometimes, even the mention of having a *'plan'* can provide a false sense of security, as people may rightly or wrongly think that the plan is more detailed than it is or will work as documented

The idea of the strategy and plan is not to try and catch people out or make the participants feel uncomfortable but to provide confidence in the guidance available, and more importantly, where there is too much reliance on assumptions that may have been made, as we discussed in *Chapter 2, Actions.*

In *Chapter 13, Lessons,* we explored isomorphic learning and the correlations between disparate incidents. As we have identified, major incidents can be caused by a multitude of things. Complex and large-scale events may be driven by a chain reaction of systematic process failings.

I believe when broken down to their lowest denominator, organizations are the same, irrespective of whether it is a small business or multinational enterprise. They all have dependencies on people, buildings, technology, as well as the individuals and organizations they trade with.

When considering the impact of an event, we can break these core scenarios down to:

- Loss or access to key location(s)

- Loss or access to the key system(s)

- Loss or access to a key resource(s)

- Loss or access to a key supplier(s)

When examining the proactive *'Questions,'* we should identify the *'what if'* and *'so what'* associated with each of these and *'how'* and *'why'* something could go wrong. Do not wait until an incident has occurred before establishing the why. If you have applied *'Diligence'* thoroughly, this should be known; hence, you can recommend actions to protect and recover each of these items.

The onus is on the organization to identify the key locations, systems, resources, and suppliers through business continuity processes.

When considering resources, this extends to people, data, and equipment. For people, this should consider the reliance on specific skills and knowledge that may be retained by a few people, as well as the widespread unavailability of people for a sustained period.

Exercising the crisis response

Many plans or tests often take a simplistic approach. Organizations may choose to perform walkthroughs or tabletop exercises of the plans. While these types of activities can undoubtedly help participants to understand key actions, roles, and responsibilities, it is not at a level and magnitude that will enable the organization to test its resilience of the organization.

Walkthroughs and tabletop exercises are essential in providing awareness of the strategy and plan, but they are performed in safe environments, with tea and coffee and refreshments offered. They take place when people are in their normal environment and have normal reactions to events. They are unlikely to revert to survival mode in the same way that they will when they are under a stressful situation and duress. People will be unlikely to remember what they did or how they reacted from just a tabletop exercise.

People can tend to make sweeping statements about what they think will happen rather than proving what will happen. It is relatively easy to state that *"we will just recover from backup tapes"* in the event of catastrophic IT failure or outage. The next question we need to ask is – *"can you prove it"*? Unless such statements have been verified, they are just assumptions, and I have already discussed the dangers of those!

For example, let us cast our mind back to the case study in *Chapter 11, Justice,* concerning the Colonial Pipeline ransomware attack. You will recall that the CEO stated that they had performed tabletop exercises and did not have a specific plan or strategy for dealing with ransomware or how they would manage an event that would necessitate the shutting down of the pipeline. Potentially the first time that executives had been placed under so much pressure was in a real-life event.

It is, therefore, important that exercises mimic real life as much as possible so that people can experience how it feels, how they would cope, and how they might refine their plans.

Of course, we do not want to jump straight into a complex scenario if it is the first time that the incident and crisis management team have participated in an exercise or it is the first time that they have seen the plan.

Exercising just one element of the plan to a deeper level can be more effective than trying to exercise the whole thing in one go.

As maturity increases, different elements of the strategy and plan can be looked at in unison to ensure no contradictory statements or misunderstandings in the actions required and assumptions being made.

An example of how beneficial large-scale exercises can be in demonstrating preparedness was highlighted in the previous *chapter*. You will note that the depth, breadth, and scale of the exercise and the confidence that it enabled were performed over the course of several years. And hence, developing resilience is a long-term commitment and essential for long-term survivability.

It is rare to have an event of such a magnitude warrant a business-wide crisis response that does not cause some significant detriment or impact to customers and partners across the supply chain. A byproduct of the digital era and global pandemic is the fragility of the worldwide supply chain in the delivery of *'just-in-time'* products and services.

To enable resilience of the supply chain, it will therefore be a necessity to plan for an incident that has an upstream and downstream impact on the supply chain and which parties need to be involved in verifying and closing some of the broader assumptions that may be outside the immediate control of the organization.

The language we utilize to communicate the output of an exercise is also a contributing factor to how people engage. Rather than stating that an exercise is a pass or a failure, rewording this as *'Lessons'* learned and *'Opportunities'* for improvement generates a more positive response from people.

In *Chapter 22, 'Underdog'* we further explore the fragility of the supply chain .

Conclusion

In this chapter, we have explored how to prioritize and exercise the crisis response by considering the type of scenarios. I identified that resilience is enabled by considering the overall culture of the organization and providing confidence to all those that will be involved in the incident and crisis response. The objective is to increase maturity in the overall crisis response as a measure of resilience.

Reflection

- How does the overall incident and crisis management approach complement and support the business continuity program? Have you identified the key locations, systems, resources, and suppliers needed to maintain core products and services, and for how long?

- Have you identified the *'severe but plausible'* scenarios that could impact the organization, and to what level? I'll ask again just to be sure – what is your worst-case scenario – has this been agreed upon with top management, and have they shown a level of commitment to building a resilience strategy that goes up to and beyond the worst-case? Your answer should influence the roadmap I discussed in the previous chapter on *'Resilience.'*

- Have you identified the upstream and downstream impact of a significant incident and taken the opportunity to include customers, partners, and suppliers in your resilience efforts?

- What is the extent of your current test and exercise program, and how are you delivering confidence in the viability of plans?

- Are you also an active participant in customer, partner, and supplier tests and exercises, so they may also determine their level of resilience?

Suggested actions

- Thinking back to *Chapter 2 'Action'* and the need to guide people on the priorities and decisions required, create a test and exercise strategy and program that enables you to prove each element of the plan. Consider how you can build these to inject more realism into the exercises to address the coping mechanisms and stressors that people may encounter. As identified, the exercises should aim to remove assumptions in favor of facts systematically.

- Document the outcome of each test and exercise, identifying lessons and opportunities for improvement at every stage.

- As maturity in the exercise regime grows, extend the remit to include other interested parties.

In the next chapter, I shall discuss why *'Time'* really is of the essence during a major incident and why every minute counts.

CHAPTER 21
Time

T = TIME

"Time and tide wait for no man."

—*Geoffrey Chaucer, English Author*

People tend to overestimate the power of a threat and underestimate the time they must respond.

We cannot alter the passage of time or change history, but we can embrace it and learn from it. We have identified that both hindsight and foresight are powerful tools that enable us to make choices in the present

We cannot slow time down and often wish we had more. Time is a precious commodity that should not be wasted.

Structure

In this chapter, I shall discuss the following:

- Time is of the essence

- The past

- The present

- The future

Objectives

In this chapter, we shall explore why time is of the essence in a major incident and why we need to be cognizant of the actions, decisions, and consequences that we make in that time. As we have discussed in previous chapters and as we share and explore further in the book, our objective is to determine an accurate and logical sequence of events that can be time-stamped and verified as evidence.

Time is of the essence

Since the beginning of the millennium, we have become less accepting of downtime and expect services to be available anytime, anywhere, from any device. The speed of digital services and how the information is shared are not confined by countries or boundaries.

During a major incident, time is of the essence. The longer we wait, the higher the impact. We cannot afford to let the passage of time be to the detriment of the actions we must take. Although memory fades, the actions of organizations will not be forgotten.

As I identified, personalities and strong characters matter to prevent people from being paralyzed in fear of making a mistake. Conversely, those that promote rational thinking ensure actions are methodical and well thought out. It ultimately requires strong and charismatic leadership to lead others through a crisis.

The past

The information collated and shared through public inquiries, post-incident reviews, and the stories we read in the media all contribute to our understanding of the past.

By reviewing and establishing the cause and effect of an incident, we can determine that a major incident is often the result of an accumulation of actions and decisions that were made in the past, and the effect is how these manifested themselves in the present.

It is through *'Diligence'* and the establishment and reporting of *'Facts'* that have enabled to identify *'Lessons.'*

The power of hindsight is a valuable tool, but only if used to impact and inform the future. Foresight can be equally powerful, but only if we actively apply the *'Knowledge'*, we have gained. The *'Opportunity'* relies on what we do next.

The present

When we have information and knowledge at our disposal that has the power to change our perception, that enables us to think and act differently, and that allows us to affect the outcome of what is to come, we must think about how what we do in the present influences the future.

We waste opportunities when we fail to act on the knowledge and intelligence we hold. The case studies highlighted show how each of these wasted opportunities afforded us the ability to change the outcome. While we do not know how exactly this would have changed the trajectory of the incident, we can at least acknowledge that the repercussions of inaction are higher than some actions.

We can make excuses and state we do not have time, but we all have the same hours in the day, and it is our gift to prioritize that time.

Each wasted hour or day that passes is now confined to the past. If mistakes are made, or wrong decisions are made, we can acknowledge and be available to fix and prioritize what we did.

- We can reduce the time to act and decide through better information, *'Knowledge'*, and automation.

- We can reduce the time to recover through the *'Strategy'* that we deploy and establish *'Resilience'* by testing our level of preparedness.

- We can reduce the time to provide *'Justice'* to those that need it by not impeding *'Investigations'* and actively contributing to establishing a detailed and factual timeline.

Make the most of the time you have, and make it count. There is no time like the present to enable change.

The future

The future has not happened yet. This means that anything is possible. While so many variables can alter the course of what is to come, they are directly in our control. This includes the people we liaise with personally and professionally, the information we openly share, and the information we choose to hide. We have already shown how each action has a consequence, and each interaction can cause a chain reaction.

A key opportunity for the future is to help people visualize and contribute to what a successful crisis response may look like or how resilience can be achieved. This helps to create a new mental model with a plan and roadmap of how you will get there. This can help reduce the fear and trepidation and the task size ahead. This is not a short-term fix but a long-term vision for the organization that enables them to consider the art of the possible, which is inspiring for people. As I shall discuss more in *Chapter 23, Victory,* people tend to want to have something that they can get behind and believe in.

A lesson in foresight is as valuable as a lesson in hindsight. The one thing we know to be accurate, and what we can take away from the case studies and anecdotes, is that history will repeat itself if left unchanged.

One question we need to ask ourselves is, are we collectively building a future for the better or worse? Are we taking sufficient accountability for what lies ahead?

Conclusion

In this chapter, we have explored why time is a critical factor in the overall crisis response and why actions and decisions need to be considered wisely since, once made, they cannot be undone. The need to proactively consider and manage time goes beyond the initial response to consider the full end-to-end incident lifecycle.

Reflection

- This is a simple but poignant question and one that may take a little more introspection. Are you making the most of your time?

- Is the organization learning from the past and taking positive action in the present to determine the longevity and resilience of the future?

Actions

- Thinking back to the resilience roadmap and strategy I discussed in the previous two chapters, take steps to bring this to life by visualizing how each step of the journey will benefit the organization and people.

In the next chapter, I will discuss the issue of supply chain resilience and why the *'Underdog'* should never be estimated.

CHAPTER 22
Underdog

U = UNDERDOG

"He who is not courageous enough to take risks will accomplish nothing in life."

—*Muhammed Ali, U.S. Sports Figure*

Never underestimate the plight of the underdog.

They have nothing to lose and everything to gain.

Structure

In this chapter, I shall discuss

- A tale of two companies

- Survival of the fittest

- Disrupted or disrupter?

Objectives

The aim of this chapter is to highlight complacency and to be mindful of the competition, as well as the will and determination to succeed our competitors. People generally favor the underdog in their ability to exceed all expectations. Having a good understanding of upstream and downstream impact is a key facet of resilience.

A tale of two companies

I am sure you have heard the biblical tale of '*David and Goliath.*' Let us use it as a metaphor for the modern era to look at two organizations.

Goliath (*Company A*) was significant, robust, and a giant amongst his peers. People had grown dependent on Goliath to protect them, as he was considered too big to fail. But Goliath was not there for the people. He was willing to take huge risks to better himself and fight the competition. He believed in his strength so much that he got complacent. When he saw David on the horizon, he just laughed and ignored him.

David (*Company B*) did not have the power of Goliath. He lacked experience and resources, and no one expected him to be able to beat Goliath. They, too, ignored him.

David was confident in his abilities, was quick on his feet, and saw an '*Opportunity*'. He was able to maneuver quickly, to outperform and defeat Goliath.

Goliath did not see this coming; by the time he noticed, it was too late. Goliath crashed heavily, the people lost faith in him, and without their support, he could not rise back up. The giant was no more.

So, what can we learn from this?

Our role is not to stamp out or impede the underdog but to pull up a seat at the table and invite them to discuss evolving strategies and tactics which cater to strength, agility, and speed, for we have a common goal to achieve.

Survival of the fittest

British Naturalist *Charles Darwin*[1] coined the phrase *'survival of the fittest'* with his theory of evolution. This suggested that organisms that best adjust to their environment are the most successful in surviving within their ecosystem. This can vary with the forces at play around them and how they grow and mature.

Let's consider this in the modern era. Organizations need to consider how the external social, economic, and geopolitical factors will impact how they will adapt to change, now and into the future, to remain relevant amongst their peers.

Disrupted or disrupter?

There is a lot of hype about the rapid pace of technology change and whether you are a *'disrupter'* such as Uber, Netflix, and Amazon, or the *'disrupted'* such as Nokia, Blackberry, and Kodak. The latter being organizations that failed to react quickly enough to changes in market conditions and consumer demands and paid the price.

At the time of this book's publication, the most downloaded and popular application was TikTok[2]. Launched internationally in 2017, TikTok generated an estimated $4.6 billion in revenue in 2021 and amassed over 1 billion users. The number of users is expected to double by the end of 2022. This is a testament to the power of social networking globally.

Research conducted by Constellation[3] identified that 52% of the Fortune 500 have been merged, acquired, bankrupt, or fallen off the list since 2000.

The research highlighted that this was not due to the pace of technological change but the shift in how new business models is created.

There is a risk that many organizations will not exist in a meaningful way in the next 10-15 years unless there is a willingness and desire for organizations to disrupt themselves and create wholesale change.

---

1   Charles Darwin, On the Origin of Species, 1864

2 Mansor Iqbal, Business of Apps, TikTok Revenue & Usage Statistics 19th August 2022, https://www.businessofapps.com/data/tik-tok-statistics/ (retrieved 21st August 2022)

3 Ray Wang, Disrupting Digital Business: Create an Authentic Experience in a Peer-to-Peer Economy, July 2016.

This is not simply about reacting to changes in technology and innovation but anticipating and reacting to societal changes and global threats that are happening on an unprecedented scale.

The reality is that organizations are often too slow to act or slow to implement the necessary changes. For larger organizations, in particular, transformation programs can take years to implement and quickly become outdated, as technology has already moved on. Organizations often struggle to think beyond the here and now or make the required cultural shift.

A change in mindset and culture is required. This includes removing the notion that *'it will never happen to me,'* *'it is not my problem,'* or *'it is not my sector'* mentality. Events have shown that no organization or community is immune to disruption.

And as per the tale of David and Goliath, sometimes the bigger you are, the harder you fall.

There is no value in being the last one standing when all the others have failed. We are stronger together when we work and collaborate in unison.

Consider that change happens to us while disruption happens within us. People may deal with change as a psychological process, and organizational change management is not always adapted to lead change within people. Instead, they focus on how they will manage the operational aspects of the change and not how they will help people adapt to what is on the horizon.

As I shall discuss in the next chapter, people want to be led, guided, and inspired. This is a core principle that organizations must consider if they want people to go on the journey with them.

Conclusion

This chapter explored the will and determination of the underdog. In particular, their ability to deliver proactive change and win hearts and minds. This can occur when organizations lose sight of their vision and objective or their appreciation of the competitive landscape.

Reflection

- Think about your organization. Are you a disrupter or one of the disrupted? How do you know if the products and services are still relevant, and how will the organization need to adapt and change?

- Who are your core competitors, and are you paying enough attention to the start-ups and scale-ups in your industry and the investment they need or are receiving? How fast are they growing in their markets, and have they found a niche that others have not?

- What is the organization's view of small and medium enterprises, is your role in helping or hindering their growth, and is there a mutual benefit to be gained by working together, especially in times of crisis? People will remember what you did and why as a responsible business.

Suggested actions

- Thinking back to the *'Resilience'* roadmap and *'Strategy'* I discussed in previous chapters, ensure that this includes changes in market forces. A great example is how certain events, such as the COVID19 global pandemic, deliver seismic shifts. In particular, how people's attitudes are changing and evolving when it comes to hybrid working and how collaboration tools enable people to communicate and share information in innovative ways.

In the next chapter, I shall explore why it is important to celebrate a *'Victory'*, no matter how small it may seem.

CHAPTER 23
Victory

V = VICTORY

"Forewarned is forearmed; to be prepared is half the victory."

—*Miguel de Cervantes, Spanish Author*

In a crisis, we can fixate on the negative, often forgetting about the tremendous daily effort to plan, prepare and respond to incidents.

So, it is essential to celebrate the victories, no matter how big or small.

Structure

In this chapter, I shall discuss the following:

- Protecting the castle

- Understanding human needs

- Positive reinforcement

Objectives

This chapter aims to highlight the work that incident response teams provide end-to-end to reduce the probability or impact of an incident. Often, we concentrate our effort on the attention-grabbing headlines without fully exploring how such incidents may materialize. Therefore, our objective is to consider the triangulation and availability of information to make informed decisions and how accurate that may be.

Protecting the castle

Quite often, when thinking of an organization and how they operate in siloes, we think of a castle and moat analogy, where the organization is fixated on protecting everything in the castle by preventing unauthorized access from anyone outside.

So, imagine your role is to defend the castle and everyone inside, for these are the loyal subjects you need to protect from harm.

You have invested heavily in fortifying the perimeter and may have multiple layers of defense.

But you have adversaries outside who are relentless in their quest to gain access. They have worked hard to understand the physical and logical vulnerabilities and how these can be exploited. Unknown or unresolved vulnerabilities provide an advantage to the opposition.

They have tried ramming the gates and circling the edge to find a back door or unguarded entrance.

Often, they will try impersonating someone from within, or they will gain their trust to follow behind them. They may have even coerced someone to give them access because they understand the issues and stress people may face. This has led to potential resentment as the subjects become tired and wearisome.

But each time the adversaries try and gain access, and you block, it is a victory. You learn from their tactics and plan how to defend better next time.

You can also enroll the help of people inside the castle to be your lookouts and identify suspicious behavior. But you must not scold them if they miss something because they are less likely to want to help again in the future. Instead, you offer them more guidance and remind them of their significant role in defending the castle. This allows them to feel valued.

Sometimes the adversaries come at you with new tools and weapons, which may take you off-guard, and you learn from them as you develop your strategy to counteract them.

Each time you win, it wounds them slightly, and they need to regroup, strategize, and try something new. This costs them time, resources, and effort, especially the stronger they become at pre-empting what is to come and how you need to defend yourselves

The battle can often feel exhausting, and there may be no end as attackers continue to evolve their tactics, but each maneuver and block is a win.

But you are never alone, for there are other castles in the kingdom. You trade with these castles and kingdoms, grow, and jointly prosper. With the information you now jointly share, you are better prepared and more confident in the resilience that you collectively have.

I use this as an analogy, but it is not fiction. This is how our ancestors evolved from the past to the present. The victors told heroic stories that became legends. Granted, some stories may have been embellished, and they did not have the mechanisms to record and verify facts accurately, so we might never know the truth behind such stories, but the stories of deviance and victories give people hope.

People tend to react well to stories, as they are easy to remember and can be retold. As we have also identified, people tend to favor the '*Underdog*,' and the hero in the story overcomes the adversary.

Understanding human needs

Real life is no Hollywood movie – sometimes it can be worse, but people need to feel reassured since safety and '*Wellbeing*' are basic human needs.

This forms part of *Maslow's Hierarchy of Needs*[1], in which the psychologist argued that basic needs must be met first for people to operate to their maximum and better themselves.

These levels include:

- **Psychological needs**: Vital for survival (food, water, air, shelter).

- **Safety and security needs**: Vital for control and order (employment, financial security, health and wellness, safety from accident and injury).

- **Love and belonging needs**: Vital for emotional relationships (family, friends, intimate relationships, social groups).

- **Self-esteem needs**: Vital for respect and appreciation (confidence, connections with others, need for individuality).

- **Self-actualization needs**: Vital for personal growth and fulfilling potential (creativity, potential, and purpose).

Psychological and safety are described as the basic needs that must be met. The fulfillment of these requirements is an indicator of happiness. People will be motivated in unusual ways and put a higher importance on achieving these needs.

The exact needs can easily be applied to an organization in that resilience and security are part of the basic building blocks of the organization, and an organization cannot achieve its full potential and growth without this function. It is core to the success of the organization. An effective and efficient crisis response helps to rebalance and protect these needs when something impacts these areas to ensure they are appropriately safeguarded. This, ultimately, is what defines our resilience.

Positive reinforcement

Quite often, business continuity, crisis management, and cybersecurity are portrayed in a negative light. They are associated with the terrible things that happen, and for many, the first time they hear about these functions is when a major incident has occurred. They are associated with the people that say *"no,"* the naysayers, and the doom-mongers. It is perhaps no wonder that people find it challenging to understand the actual value and importance of these functions.

The industry utilizes a unique language, often difficult for people to understand and occasionally sensationalist. This can often be intimidating for people.

---

1   Abraham Maslow, A Theory of Human Motivation, 4 July 1943, https://www.academia.edu/9415670/A_Theory_of_Human_Motivation_Abraham_H_Maslow_Psychological_Review_Vol_50_No_4_July_1943 (retrieved 30 July 2022)

Negative language is often used to convince people that they should care about cybersecurity and resilience, but the negativity surrounding the subject can leave people alienated and confused.

People are typically more motivated by positive and inclusive language. This means changing people's perceptions and interests. So rather than focusing on all the things people do wrong, we need to concentrate on everything they do right.

Using positive language and reinforcement can help people to see the wider value that these functions provide in delivering a protective layer around the organization, which can help people associate how the functions are helping meet those basic needs.

Building trust and transparency and celebrating the positive cultural change that comes with a suitable resilience strategy helps the organization make more informed decisions.

This needs to have *'People'* right at the center since the success or otherwise of the organization is linked to the people that work there and the level of investment they have in the organization.

This needs to be a top-down effort delivered with *'Gravitas'* so people can see why this subject is so important. This potential cultural change in emphasis needs to be given as a long-term, genuine commitment rather than a short-term campaign to improve awareness.

People need to see it, to *'Believe'* it.

Conclusion

The aim of this chapter is to provide a realization that our focus needs to be outward as well as inward facing when it comes to resilience and strategizing. It is important for people to be able to recognize victories and to use proactive reinforcement to increase awareness and build trust.

Reflection

- Consider how some of the resilience and crisis management functions are portrayed in your organization. Are they associated with negative things, and do people only hear about them when bad things go wrong?

- What can you do to change the perception? Remember what I discussed in *Chapter 16, Opportunity* about how we need to change negatives into positives? A key part of this is how you describe the value and benefit that resilience provides, not just for the organization but for the people. How is this helping to meet their basic needs for safety and security?

- How are you celebrating the victories? Do you have stories that can become organizational legends? Who are the heroes and heroines in your story, and how can you promote them? Remember what I said about identifying those people and leaders who demonstrate *Gravitas*– utilize these people to elevate and inspire people.

Suggested actions

- Thinking back to the resilience roadmap and strategy I discussed in previous chapters, ensure that this includes positive reinforcement and actions. Identify what needs to be done to win hearts and minds.

- Thinking back to the action plan I discussed in *Chapter 2, Action*, how will people know when they have achieved their objectives? Help people to envisage what the outcomes will look and feel like.

- Keep people apprised of each victory and how the organization's investment enables the organization to demonstrate resilience.

In the next chapter, we shall discuss the importance of *'Wellbeing'* and the imperative of managing the stressors that people may be facing.

CHAPTER 24
Wellbeing

Emotional resilience and wellbeing are crucial in times of crisis and are one of the basic needs we need to protect, as discussed in the previous chapter.

People tend to work longer hours and are often under increased stress. Not just from work but from whatever is happening in their personal life.

Structure

In this chapter, I shall discuss the following:

- Maintaining wellbeing in a crisis

- Managing the stressors

- Establishing emotional resilience

- Case study 6: India's most prominent corporate fraud

- Case study 7: The first global influenza pandemic in 41 years

- Large-scale industrial action

- Finding your path

- Dealing with trauma

- Recognizing trauma in others

Objectives

The aim of this chapter is to consider the overall culture of the organization and how this enables us to have a sense of wellbeing in how we perceive and operate in a crisis. Stressors can manifest in different ways and can be extenuated in a crisis. It is important to not only manage the wellbeing of those involved in the management of a major incident but also to consider your own emotional needs. For incident and crisis leaders, they are often immersed in every aspect of the incident, and it can often feel relentless, as we shall explore in the next case studies. Having a wellbeing program is not just essential for the safety of welfare of people but also to ensure that people have mechanisms to deal with the effects of stressors and trauma that they may experience.

Maintaining wellbeing in a crisis

Wellbeing is intrinsically linked to what is best for that individual, which means that it is not one-size-fits-all and needs to be adaptable. People need to feel empowered about determining what will meet their needs without this being forced upon them.

This requires a strong and empathetic leader to recognize the stressors and change behavior that may be manifesting.

Sometimes it can just be about ensuring that people are taking a break or attending to their personal needs. It indicates why flexible working has become so important with how, when, and where people work. It provides the empowerment and self-fulfillment that people may need to manage other aspects of their lives.

This is more than just doing the right thing; it is a business imperative too. Managing the needs of people and their success means you are also managing the organization's needs.

Managing the stressors

Stressors can be triggered by several things, including social, economic, and geo-political risks at a global level and the type of personal stressors that come with day-to-day life, which will be different for every person. Those stressors can often be amplified during major or traumatic events.

There is a difference between passing stress, which can be short-term and in response to a specific incident, and chronic stress. This can develop over a prolonged period and impact people's mental health and wellbeing, and thus their performance and productivity. This makes them vulnerable to making mistakes or targets for manipulation by attackers.

As a result of the COVID 19 pandemic, there has been a significant rise in insider threats. This can be attributed to several factors - the anxiety associated with lack of information and uncertainty at the outset of the pandemic, through to concerns over illness, bereavement, or redundancy.

While much of the population will feel those concerns, additional factors increase the insider threat. This includes the need for information workers to work remotely, potentially utilizing new devices, collaboration tools, and methods of communication, and challenges of sharing and oversharing the information.

In addition, front-line workers, such as emergency services, manufacturers, and distributors, were under increased pressure to maintain the operational delivery of services, potentially putting their safety and welfare at risk.

While most insider threats are non-malicious, people can be more prone to make mistakes or fall into fraud if they are feeling stressed or overwhelmed. This is how vulnerabilities can be exploited by accident or through adversaries. If we understand the stressors and the triggers that may impact people, we can take proactive actions to prevent a problem before it escalates. We can also ensure that we meet the minimum psychological and safety needs that are required for those individuals.

It is another reason the '*people first always*' mantra is essential to everything we do, as it creates an environment that enables a positive mindset.

Establishing emotional resilience

As discussed in *Chapter 16, Opportunity*, where we explored the importance of seizing opportunities, with the benefit of hindsight, I can now look back and affectionately call 2009 my year of crisis.

Back then, I was working for a large global service provider and experienced three major events, running back-to-back for an entire year. It was relentless and tiring, but I felt like I was in my element. I was put in situations that I had never experienced before; people were looking to me for answers, and it required me to think on my feet, and as much as I hate to use cliches, it also required me to think outside of the box.

Let me summarize these for you:

- India's most prominent corporate fraud

- The first global influenza pandemic in 41 years

- Large-scale industrial action

In the spirit of sharing, I will treat the first two as case studies since these were major events that also played out in the public domain. Rather than generic lessons, I share my experiences from being directly involved in the management of these incidents.

Case study 6

India's most prominent corporate fraud:

Case study 6
Satyam Corporate Fraud
India, 2009
Summary of Incident
Satyam Computer Services was an Indian partner being utilized in the global rollout of six new Data Centers for a financial services customer. Satyam's role was to provide remote infrastructure management and a network operations center.
On 9th January 2009, the chairperson of Satyam resigned from the Board after confessing[1] to severe accounting irregularities that had accrued over the cause of several years.

---

1 Satyam Chairman resignation letter submitted to stock exchanges (9 January 2009): https://www. sec.gov/Archives/edgar/data/1106056/000114554909000025/u00107exv99w2.htm retrieved 12 July 2022

The formal investigation by independent parties would identify profits that did not exist, 13,000 people being paid salaries that did not exist, and cash at the Bank that did not exist. All of which had been designed to inflate the share price and make the company more attractive to investors and prospective customers.

Meanwhile, large sums of money were being embezzled to fund property and other lucrative transactions through money laundering. It is estimated that the fraud amounted to c.$700 million.

The fraud would come to be referred to as *'India's Enron'* and was just one year after the global financial crash.

Analysis of the incident

- When the announcement by the Chairman was first made, other senior management officials tried to distance themselves, stating that they were unaware, and suspended other members of the Board.

- Slowly the communications dried up, employees of Satyam stopped being paid, and holds were placed on Satyam's company's finances and accounts by the Indian law enforcement and investigators.

- Organizations working with Satyam started to terminate contracts and suspend engagements.

- What ensued was an 8-week intensive program to try and work out how to take on a global service without any network, infrastructure, staff, or procedures. This had to be achieved without the loss of service in a highly regulated environment.

- A team of people consisting of program managers, lawyers and commercial advisors, solution architects, consultants, and technology specialists from across the globe worked around the clock to design and implement the services, thinking of novel ways to limit the impact.

- My role was to create the invocation plan – a step-by-step guide listing the thresholds and triggers by which we could legally step in and take control of the services. This included a timeline for what needed to happen, by when, and by whom.

- I liken it to the *Goldilocks* project – where everything had to be just right – invoke the plan too soon or too late, and things could have had disastrous consequences. Remember what I was saying about *'Actions'* and understanding how each action or inaction can create a chain reaction and ripple effect?

- When we got to the point where invocation was inevitable, the crisis was averted in April 2009, when the Indian firm *Tech Mahindra* acquired what was left of Satyam with a commitment to rebrand and rebuild the services.

Lessons we can learn from this
• This is a notable example of a '*Near Miss*' because of another company stepping into to buy Satyam, the organization I worked for never had to fully invoke and enact the plan to take on the global service.
• Despite this, there was the realization of how much trust is placed in third parties, especially those deemed partners.
• The level of access and privilege to technology infrastructure and applications meant that it was not a simple task to be able to just scize control of the network and infrastructure. The opposite was true - they could have locked us out of the network, changed permissions, or deleted or exfiltrated data. One of the extreme actions we discussed would have been physically removing network cables from servers had it gotten to that point. Not a simple task when considering how to get everything back online and onto a new network with minimal impact!
• The key lesson is retaining oversight when authorizing and verifying physical and logical access and privileges to any third party and performing regular independent audits. Irrespective of any third parties involved in delivering the service, the organization still retains overall accountability for the services and ensures these are being delivered as expected.
• This is an area I shall come back to in *Chapter 27, Zero Trust*, where everything needs to be successfully verified before we can trust. This is not an area that can simply be taken for granted.

Case study 7

The first global influenza pandemic in 41 years

As the first incident ended, I was on to the next one.

Case study 7
H1NI Pandemic
Global, 2009-10
Summary of Incident
An outbreak of new respiratory infection was first detected in Mexico in March 2009.
By April 2009, the *World Health Organization* publicly declared the 'novel A (H1N1) 2009' to be a public health emergency of international concern, and by June 2009, a global influenza pandemic was declared[2].

2 Jennifer Nuzzo, A closer look at the WHO Pandemic Declaration, John Hopkins Center for Health Security (11 June 2019), https://www.centerforhealthsecurity.org/our-work/publications/a-closer-look-at-the-who-pandemic-declaration retrieved 17 July 2022)

The pandemic spread everywhere and reached all continents within a brief period.

By October / November 2009, public concern over the pandemic had declined. Yet, the pandemic virus continued to circulate the globe, and by August 2010, the H1N1 virus had run its course and now follows the behavior of a seasonal influenza virus.

In June 2012, the U.S *Center for Disease Control* (*CDC*) estimated[3] that there had been between 151,700 and 575,400 people perished worldwide during the first year the virus circulated.

Analysis of the incident

- Despite the organization that I worked for having high-level pandemic plans, they were out of date and lacked the level of detail required to operate across continents.

- Many central government and local legislation were conflicting and changing rapidly. It became apparent that a single global plan would not be sufficient.

- Committing to a strategy and plan to continue to deliver services to the same service level agreements became increasingly difficult, especially as more people became ill and had to take time off work to isolate or to t care of children and other loved ones.

- The changing landscape and issues of dealing with varying government policies were brought to the forefront in June 2009 when the Malaysian government decided to close specific facilities at the first laboratory-confirmed cases of H1N1, to contain the virus. That decision would also mean the closure of the entire Asia-Pacific service desk, which had to act as a follow-the-sun service with the Americas and Europe, Middle East, and Africa (EMEA) regions.

Lessons we can learn from this

- Now, I know what you are thinking. The title states this is the first influenza pandemic in 41 years, but I know there have been other pandemics – and you will be right.

- Between 2002 and 2003, a serious coronavirus outbreak known as severe acute respiratory syndrome (SARS), originating from China, quickly spread around the globe.

- Another coronavirus outbreak occurred in 2012, known as the Middle East respiratory syndrome (MERS), which originated in Saudi Arabia.

---

3 First Global Estimates of 2009 H1N1 Pandemic Mortality released by CDC (25 June 2012), https://www.cdc.gov/flu/spotlights/pandemic-global-estimates.htm, retrieved 17

- Just 7 years later, we would have the latest coronavirus – COVID 19, which we have all become familiar with over the last few years.

- Even when dealing with the H1N1 influenza virus, there was extraordinarily little information relating to previous pandemics to work from, and I had to locate this information myself.

- Fast forward 10 years from 2009, to the start of the COVID 19 pandemic in 2019, and not much changed. Little in the way of guidance could have prepared us for what was to come. Issues with information sharing across countries and medical professions continued to lead to conflicting information and advice on containment and what steps individuals and organizations should take to protect themselves. There was confusion over changing policies and advice that left people despondent.

- Despite several pandemics in a relatively short time, little has been learned.

While still dealing with the H1N1 pandemic came my third major incident of the year and another event that would last several months.

Large-scale industrial action

After a particularly turbulent year, following the economic downturn and financial crash of 2008, the organization I worked for was forced to make large-scale redundancies. This equated to c.1000 people within the UK.

As expected, many people were in turmoil as thousands of people were told their role was at risk. While they sat and awaited the outcome, the two trade unions in situ called for multiple strike actions across various locations and a work-to-rule – which meant no additional work hours or overtime. So, if your contract states that you work 8 hours per day, which is all people were told to work, with no grace and favor or down tools and go home.

As you can expect, as a service organization, there is a heavy reliance on people working shifts and overtime to deal with incidents and change requests. This is a welcome addition to their wage and job structure for many. But, when faced with the prospect of no job and with the rallying cries of the trade unions, this stopped.

So, while HR and management teams negotiated, the commercial teams were trying to manage customer contracts and relationships, especially in the event of a failing service level and the prospect of penalties and termination.

My role was twofold: to monitor changes in employee communications, what locations may be impacted by strikes, and to monitor critical services proactively to ensure core services were managed effectively.

Each of these events highlighted that for the best will in the world, and despite proactive planning, there are multiple things outside your control, which will mean having to pivot in different directions. Sometimes, major incidents will also happen simultaneously.

While this year was exhausting, I came into a world of my own, and it highlighted the value of creative thinking and problem-solving.

Finding your path

I excelled further over the next few years, temporarily moving away from a customer-facing role, and working in governance, risk, and compliance, where I would have the opportunity to design, build and implement a corporate-wide business continuity program from the ground up.

This accumulated in the company being recognized as the first IT Service Provider to achieve ISO22301 (the international standard for Business Continuity Management Systems) for the entire organization. This entailed all customer-facing functions, such as data centers, service desks, engineering, and account teams, right through to back-office functions, such as HR, procurement, and commercial teams, and took almost three years to implement from start to finish.

I moved back into a customer-facing role and was also promoted to the head of continuity and resilience, where I had the opportunity to share all the lessons learned with customers and help them to build and implement their corporate-wide program on a similar scale. I started to be invited to share my experiences with external organizations through keynote discussions and conferences.

I had come to believe that I had the aptitude and skill to deal with an array of major incidents and issues that would come my way.

That was until my mother died suddenly in 2016.

Dealing with trauma

The day started normally.

It was Easter weekend, and I wanted to invite my mother to lunch, as our extended family had come for a visit. I called her Friday evening and left a message on her answer phone, but I did not hear back from her.

I called again in the morning and had no response.

I went to lunch as intended but was concerned that I had not heard back from her, so I drove to her apartment to see if she was OK. I had keys to her apartment, and it was normal for me to let myself in, as I did that day.

When I called out her name and had no response, I knew something was wrong.

I stepped further into her living room, expecting her to be in the bedroom. As I looked down the corridor towards her bedroom, I saw her body on the floor.

I intuitively knew she was dead through the position of her body. I will spare you the details, but I was in shock and panicked. Apart from seeing my grandmother's body in an open casket at the funeral home, I had never seen a dead body before, and this was my mother!

I did not dare to enter the room, as I had already seen enough – I banged on a neighbor's door and pleaded for help. It still fills me with guilt that I exposed this person to see my mother this way, but at the time, I did not think about it. I just needed help.

Having called the police, and an ambulance, the call center operator, stated that CPR needed to be performed until paramedics arrived. I knew it was a fruitless task, but the neighbor did this anyway. As the paramedics arrived, she was declared dead at the scene.

A friend of mine, who is also a police officer, heard our surname over the radio and asked whether he could attend the scene. I am forever grateful for this, as he took me into my neighbor's apartment while her home was searched and her body removed. Due to having died in potentially suspicious circumstances, her body was to be transferred to the coroner.

Once the initial shock had subsided, I went straight into my practical crisis management mode, thinking of all *the 'Actions'* and plans that I needed to do. It was all about *'Communication'* - contacting all her family and friends, contacting organizations she had accounts with, and considering funeral arrangements. I was very methodical in my approach, ticking each action off my list as I went and keeping a detailed account of what I had done and whom I had spoken with, just like we have discussed in this book. I did everything I could do to keep busy because when I stopped, I played the images over and over in my head.

At the end of the two weeks' compassionate leave, I still did not have a verdict from the coroner, and I still could not arrange the funeral. I was in limbo, but I needed to go back to work.

I went to my doctor to get a certificate to cover the time off work, and he started to ask me some probing questions.

I explained how I was keeping myself busy. He then exclaimed to me: *"You are not coping. I am going to extend your compassionate leave by 6 weeks, and I want you to promise me one thing… and that is to "Just Stop.""*

This was a completely alien thing to me and was not something I was used to.

I asked him what I was supposed to do, and in answer, *"I want you to do nothing – I want you to have no other concerns or worries and to just deal with the trauma and grief. Each time you start to think about your mother, I want you to experience it, not fight it and let any emotion that follows come. If you want to cry, you can, but you cannot fight or suppress it"*.

And so, I did.

It was an uncomfortable experience - not just in terms of reliving each moment when it arose, but also feeling guilty about not being at work and wondering what my colleagues thought of me.

During that period, I was finally able to lay my mother to rest, and I could see her in the funeral home looking quite different from how I had seen her last. She looked small and frail despite only being sixty-two, but I was glad to see her lying in peace.

The coroner eventually confirmed that she had died of natural causes but could not tell me if she had died instantly or whether she suffered on her own. This played heavily on my mind for quite some time. I then remembered what I tell others and what I am telling you, which is you can only deal in '*Facts*' and not speculation.

I do not share this story out of sympathy, and I share this with you because even the strongest people will hide their feelings, and sometimes you will need to be that person to recognize this and just tell them to Stop.

Recognizing trauma in others

When faced with major incidents, whether working for an organization or through personal circumstances, those involved may naturally do whatever they feel is needed, to the point of exhaustion.

It also showed me how my father had looked after many soldiers returning from war and conflict zones years earlier. Those who had witnessed or experienced great physical and mental trauma.

This reminded me of when I was studying at the Disaster and Emergency Management School. I had an opportunity to speak to another one of the students, who happened to be a Detective Sergeant in the major crimes unit. He explained that as a rooky police officer, you are never really prepared for some of the scenes that you must attend, whether that's accidents or crime scenes. Some can be quite horrific and shocking.

This can be quite difficult for some young officers and other emergency responders, but the danger is that you become desensitized to it. I asked whether people received counseling, and briefings after the things they witnessed, and he explained that, at the time, it was a case of *"man up"* and *"do your job."* He did recall one case that traumatized him deeply – the homicide of a young infant who had been abused and neglected over a sustained period. It would remind him of his children and his need to protect them from the world. He was discouraged from talking to his spouse or other officers, and it was normal to bottle things up. This could often lead to depression, anger, and other emotions that would build up over time.

For those operating constantly on the front line, whether military, emergency services, and incident responders across the public and private sectors, it can feel relentless. People can suffer from fatigue and burnout because they are never really off-duty when a major incident occurs. There is the added pressure that one mistake, or one lapse in concentration, can worsen things.

Consider the rigidity or flexibility of your organizational policies regarding HR wellbeing programs and support and the mechanisms available to assist people in the short, medium, and long term where applicable.

This also taught me the value and importance of emotional resilience, and why the perception of normality can differ from one person to another, as do their coping mechanism, when faced with an array of incidents. Anyone can fall victim to trauma, which can manifest in many ways. Severe stress can destroy lives.

Our recollection of events can also be distorted following traumatic and stressful events. We may confuse what happened to us, and may choose to vividly recall or block events in our minds. This is a key area that I discussed previously in regard to the manifestation of PTSD, and why relying on eye-witness statements rather than video-evidence can be unreliable.

This is why '*People*' and '*Empathy*' play a significant role in crisis response.

Conclusion

In this chapter we have explored some of the issues associated with major and traumatic events, and how this can manifest at different stages in life. It is imperative for the organization to have the mechanisms in place to identify and manage stressors that people may be experiencing.

Reflection

- Consider how the organization is identifying and managing the stressors people may face within their environment. How is the organization contributing or alleviating the stressors?

- Are people empowered to identify their needs, and are they supported by the organization? Do you have a range of wellbeing policies and programs that can deal with short-term and long-term requirements?

- How are you enabling people to deal with different aspects of trauma in their lives? Consider that in the case of PTSD, this can manifest at different times and will require specialist support.

- How are you managing the insider threat? In particular, are people more prone to making mistakes, or are they vulnerable targets for manipulation? What steps are you taking to manage and control the stressors that the organization may cause?

- As the incident and crisis responder within your organization, are you also addressing and evaluating your own needs and those of others?

Suggested actions

- Thinking back to *Chapter 2, Action* ensure that appropriate breaks and rest time are included in the action plan and enforced. Identify shift patterns for incidents that will take a long period to resolve or where additional resources may be required.

- Ensure there is debriefing after every incident, enabling people to address their feelings and the emotions they may have been feeling. Some people may have been placed under acute stress and or experienced trauma. Ensure that specialist support is provided beyond the end of the incident. Note that there is a difference between offering support and providing it. People may be less inclined to do this for themselves, so the organization should be proactive in this regard.

- Instigate an insider threat program. Note that this should be focused on identifying the proactive steps that the organization can take to prevent a violation before it happens. This will be a mix of people, processes, and technology. Also, remember what I said about taking a *'People'* first approach This means understanding the triggers and thresholds that may give rise to an insider threat and actively working to resolve it.

In the next chapter, we shall circle back to some of the aspects that we discussed in *Chapter 10, Investigation,* and why *'X marks the spot'*.

CHAPTER 25
X - Marks the Spot

X = X MARKS THE SPOT

"By becoming interested in the cause, we are less likely to dislike the effect."

—*Dale Carnegie, U.S. Writer & Lecturer*

The X is synonymous with positioning on a map to get to the root cause of an incident.

Like what you may expect on a pirate's treasure map, the path is never straightforward. There are obstacles and things to uncover, potentially conflicting or missing information, and the more you dig, the more complex the task may be. You might not even know what you are looking for, but you will be inclined to keep exploring with an open mind to establish what lies beneath.

There will undoubtedly be gaps as you try and put all the pieces together to make sense of what is in front of you.

Structure

In this chapter, I shall discuss the following:

- Retracing the steps to establish a timeline

Objectives

The aim of this chapter is to draw on many of the facets that have been discussed in previous chapters when determining cause and effect and how and why incidents occur. This is particularly relevant for determining what and when as a series of discreet facts.

Retracing steps to establish a timeline

The record-keeping and the '*Facts*' versus fiction we spoke about are so essential now because you may go down a rabbit hole based on the fiction, misinformation, and rumors that have surfaced. There will be times when you must retrace your steps to get back on the right path and reaffirm what you thought you knew.

As more information becomes available because of formal '*Investigations*,' there may be some trepidation and concern about what you uncover.

As crisis responders and leaders, it is our role to identify and place the position of the X for others to follow from the '*Questions*' we ask and the '*Lessons*' that we remember, which comes with the desire to pursue the truth. With this comes credibility and trust in the organization.

The case studies and public inquiries that we have examined in this book were only possible because of others '*Diligence*'; hence, our role is to do the same so that others may also learn and improve their '*Knowledge*'.

Conclusion

In this chapter, we have explored that in order to truly understand what happened and why we must be willing to retrace our steps and question the validity of our actions. Understanding conflicting timelines and actions can help to rationalize the decisions that were made so that we can build upon our resilience.

Reflection

- What is your organization's overall approach to performing root cause analysis? Is there a genuine desire to do what is needed and uncover the truth?

- Do you have mechanisms to identify how and when an incident happened? As noted in the case studies, the triggers for some events can often occur much before the actual incident itself, which is why we need to be committed to understanding why.

Suggested actions

- Think back to the action plan in *Chapter 2, Action* and the need to document the results of each action and decision made. Document this in a post-incident review report. This should focus on the actions and viewpoints of the organization and may include input from other third parties involved. Similar to the case study in *Chapter 10, Investigation* on the Grenfell Tower Fire, the investigation and report can be considered in two phases – Phase 1) to identify what, when, and how the incident happened, and Phase 2) why the incident happened in the way that it did.

- For this chapter, concentrate on documenting Phase 1. For complex incidents with multiple stakeholders, it may be prudent to utilize the help of an independent party to gather and report on the '*Facts.*' This can help to remove unintended bias or blame from the findings, as I discussed in *Chapter 11, Justice.*

Note that there were will requirements for a formal investigation in the case of an incident resulting in significant injuries or fatalities. This could also lead to civil or criminal action, so the organization must be as open and transparent as possible with each review and investigation.

But just like all good maps, you cannot plot an X without a Y, so the next chapter in the book is interrelated.

CHAPTER 26
Y-Why

Y = PRONOUNCED THE SAME AS WHY

"When we understand people; when we understand situations; when we understand what matters; when we understand the why's, the what's and the how's; when we understand the trigger of actions, we least inflict pain on ourselves and unto others."

—*Ernest Agyemang Yeboah, Ghanaian Writer & Teacher*

In the last chapter, we talked about X marking the spot in terms of understanding the incident's root cause and establishing what happened.

But that is just one part of the equation, for you cannot understand your X until you also determine your Y. They depend on each other, but X must come first.

Structure

In this chapter, I shall discuss the following:

- Performing deep analysis

- Establishing multiple lines of inquiry

- Correlating cause and effect

Objectives

The aim of this chapter is to explain why we need to be able to correlate how and why events happen so that we can alter the sands of time and prevent repeat incidents. This means that we need to critically review each aspect of the incident so that we can refine and build upon our approach.

Performing deep analysis

As we have identified through case studies and anecdotes, things do not just break, fail, or get compromised on their own. Simply stating that *'the cause of a data breach was a cyberattack'* is not enough. Several events typically triggered the incident to manifest the way it did. Hence you need to understand WHY.

There is a train of thought that if you ask *"Why"* enough times, you will start to unearth the truth.

This is often referred to as the *'5 Why's method*[1], which was first developed to establish cause-and-effect, and problem-solving in engineering and manufacturing systems.

The theory is that by the time you have asked *"Why"* five times, you will have unearthed the root cause of a problem. This technique was first developed by *Sakichi Toyoda*, a Japanese inventor, and industrialist who founded *Toyota Industries*. This method is often utilized in lean methodologies to solve complex problems, troubleshoot, or establish the root cause of incidents.

Often jumping to conclusions takes less energy and effort, and why our own unconscious bias can cloud our judgment and decision-making. It's one of the

1 Mind Tools, 5 Whys, Getting to the root of a problem quickly, https://www.mindtools.com/pages/article/newTMC_5W.htm (retrieved 28 July 2022)

reasons we need to take a rational approach to understand why and is also indicative of why it is sometimes preferable to have independent third parties assess so as not to be swayed towards a specific preconceived outcome.

Of course, this does not mean that we just stop after five times, as the reality is more complex. But the willingness to ask these probing *'Questions'* aids with *'Diligence'* and our ability to perform thorough *'Investigations.'*

This potentially highlights how we are too quick to jump to conclusions when we do not consider all the *'Facts.'* It can therefore be a simple yet effective way of verifying whether we have done enough work to analyze the circumstances and events that contributed to the incident.

Establishing multiple lines of inquiry

Just be mindful that the path is often not linear for complex incidents and problems, which may lead to multiple lines of inquiry with different parties.

Typically, this equates to a process failure, multiple missed opportunities, or an assumption that someone, somewhere, is doing something (which usually means no one is).

So, let us use an example of a cyberattack to illustrate this point. The incident may have been caused because of an attacker obtaining a backdoor into the environment, but this does not do enough to explain how and why this happened. So, by asking more questions on the *why*, we can establish that this was caused by a system misconfiguration caused by issues in change control, which could also be attributed to a lack of resources, knowledge of risk, and so on.

Correlating cause and effect

Understanding the correlation and context between *cause* and *effect* is critical here.

So now we can show why ineffective change control can lead to cyberattacks and why we need to take affirmative action to reduce the likelihood or impact of this reoccurring. This can also include the business case for why more investment in resources, training, and awareness can help to improve the end-to-end process.

If we think back to *Chapter 18, Questions*, we also highlighted the need to reflect on *"So, what"* to consider the impact. This can help us to determine whether any of the potential causes were material to the event, and if we fixed or removed one or all of those, would the outcome have been different?

So, you can see why pinpointing the *X* and establishing the *Y* go together. All the previous chapters on the importance of *'Diligence,' 'Facts,' 'Investigation,'* and *'Justice'* are all coming to fruition now. We can show the correlation of each of these elements and why a core element of our overall crisis response and management strategy relies on more than just having a plan or checklist to follow.

Conclusion

In this chapter, we have highlighted the importance of why we needed to perform all of the previous chapters and how this all contributes to managing the end-to-end response to major incidents and crises. When we have performed all previous steps in a diligent manner, we can be assured of the outcomes. This is an ongoing and iterative process, and as long as you are committed to deep learning, you will be able to build an effective crisis response.

Reflection

- What is your organization's overall approach to performing root cause analysis? Is there a genuine desire to do what is needed and uncover the truth?

- Do you have mechanisms to work backward to correlate events and search for patterns? Quite often, the case studies point to missed warning signs, inaction, lack of understanding, and other reasons why the incident manifested in the way it did. This is why I ask you to record all the reports, actions, and decisions made before, during, and after an incident. Without this information, it will take longer to understand why and compound your ability to obtain knowledge.

- Remember what I said about history repeating itself unless something changes? There may be a requirement to dig deep at this stage to break the cycle.

Suggested actions

- Linking to the previous chapter, once Phase 1 has been performed, move into Phase 2. These can be documented together or separately, depending on the scope and scale of the incident.

- The requirements to understand why should consider not just why the incident happened but why the incident took the trajectory it did. As I identified in previous chapters, you can only make decisions based on information available at the time, so carefully consider why an action or decision was made. Also, consider whether those making decisions or performing the actions were under stress, reasoning, and with the value of hindsight and would, the action has been the same. Arguably Phase 2 may take longer, and can often be subjective, which is why it must remain factual and not speculative.

- Note that in the case of an incident resulting in major injuries or fatalities, there were requirements for a formal investigation. This could also lead to civil or criminal action, so the organization must be as open and transparent as possible with each review and investigation.

As we enter the concluding chapters of this book, we shall again explore the principles of verifying trust.

CHAPTER 27
Zero Trust

Throughout this book, we have discussed the importance of establishing trust and transparency before, during, and after a crisis. You may therefore assume that this chapter is the opposite of that and that we do not trust anything, which becomes an oxymoron.

Both statements are factual, but the core difference is that we can no longer just explicitly trust. Trust needs to be earned and continuously verified to manage any threats effectively. When we consider the growing complexity of organizations and how any vulnerability can be exploited, it becomes necessary to actively manage and respond in a way that assumes that vulnerability is already being actively exploited so that organizations are not just waiting for incidents to manifest before they react.

Structure

In this chapter, I shall discuss the following:

- The principles of zero trust

- A business perspective on zero trust

- Crossing the boundary of technology and cybersecurity

Objectives

In this chapter, we shall discuss the importance of trust and how we cannot just unilaterally trust without verification. This was a key element of checking sources and establishing facts, not making assumptions or taking things at face value. It is about having a healthy level of skepticism in our ability to assess risk and resilience.

The principles of zero trust

Zero trust is sometimes considered a buzzword, but it becomes pretty straightforward when considering its principles.

Zero trust has become synonymous with designing technical and security architectures, but this applies equally well in a business environment for establishing end-to-end resilience against an array of risks and threats the organization may face. Technology is just one part of that, albeit a critical element in today's digital environment.

As we have covered in previous chapters on 'Resilience' and 'Strategy,' the underpinning mindset needs to be not if something may happen but that it will happen or is even happening right now. This removes some issues in trying to establish the likelihood of an incident. Therefore, with an assume compromise or failure mindset, our main determining factor is the scale of impact.

This is not to say that likelihood is not a crucial factor, but it means we need an open mind based on the plausibility of the incident.

Let us think about the outcome of *Chapter 18, Questions* where we considered the *'what if'* and the *'so what.'* With this information, we can determine the controls and plans needed to counteract this across all aspects of the organization.

A business perspective on zero trust

As a result of the global COVID19 pandemic, many organizations are already re-imagining themselves to be digital organizations, opening new lines of business, supply chains, and experiences for employees and consumers. To do this safely and securely requires a network of trust. This means verifying every transaction and communication explicitly to verify and validate each entry and data point until trust has been earned and proven.

This constant and dynamic assessment enables a degree of flexibility in reacting to and managing events as they occur before they turn into incidents. This is a necessary part of the *'Resilience'* that anticipates and plans for a range of *severe but plausible* threats and how to counteract them.

Many organizations will already deploy good practices regarding governance and compliance, such as segregation of duty and distinct levels of authorization. For example, it ensures that the same person who raised the invoice is not the same person who authorized it.

In the same way that we want to build trusted networks and architectures into technology, we need to do this in business processes and relationships, too, and consider how many of these could be vulnerabilities that could be exploited.

The key is that we do not want to make processes and signoffs so tricky and cumbersome that they become unusable. So, the principles are about balancing productivity and security. As much as possible, we want security and compliance to become second nature to our people, without the fear of repercussion if they make a mistake or become victims of a fraudulent scam.

As we identified, many attackers can manipulate the situation and people by taking advantage of vulnerabilities.

With the assume compromise and failure mindset, our objective is to consider this a default position and remove assumptions and gaps in the controls until we know the *'Facts.'* Of course, for many organizations, there is often a lack of resources or funding that enables us to close all gaps which need to be prioritized. This forms part of *'Diligence'* to ensure awareness and communication about the potential gap and repercussions. This enables management to decide and determine the *'Actions'* required to minimize the rise.

As we identified through previous chapters and with some of the case studies, often there is a mismatch between what is known by the people and what is communicated or understood by senior management as risks and threats are downplayed, or there is an assumption that they are already aware.

Building trusted networks within the business environment are just as crucial as building these into technology. It very much comes down to the culture of the organization and the willingness and desire to drive change.

Crossing the boundary of technology and cybersecurity

No longer can organizations just consider the security and resilience of IT infrastructure. With opportunities for digital innovation extending further into the physical and biological worlds, organizations must consider the dependencies between technology and operational networks. As organizations evolve their business models and look to take advantage of innovations, the environments are likely to utilize robotics combined with augmented and mixed reality and artificial intelligence.

This fusion, known as the *internet of everything*, is an ever-expanding ecosystem of digital connectivity and intelligent technologies that enables enhanced consumer and employee experiences and engagement. In parallel, it introduces additional risk and attacks vectors that can be exploited because of increased vulnerabilities.

This intersection requires us to consider digital security and safety combined, whereas the traditional need for confidentiality, integrity, and availability also requires us to build for quality, endurance, and reliability.

To be safe and secure in this hybrid world, you must start from a position that assumes you are neither safe nor secure.

We must therefore design for and assume failure by thinking of the myriad ways in which it could be physically and logically accessed by exploiting vulnerabilities. Having an assume compromise/failure mentality requires that safety and security controls be deployed.

Forging new links between the physical and digital worlds dramatically increases the scope of enterprise security and safety. This is the next step in the evolution of zero-trust, where we re-imagine a world without boundaries that enables us to operate end-to-end to explore the art of the possible.

Organizations can grow and thrive if continuity and resilience are embedded and considered basic needs.

Conclusion

In this chapter and throughout this book, we have explored that true resilience comes from understanding where the organization resides in terms of the overall supply-chain ecosystem. As more people and organizations become digitally connected and explore new ways of collaboration and innovation, establishing a trusted network is essential.

Reflection

- Is your organization embracing the zero-trust mindset?

- Is your organization centered on the principles of establishing a verified network of trust inside and outside of the organization to demonstrate resilience for interested parties?

Suggested actions

- Thinking back to the resilience and strategy roadmap we discussed in previous chapters, identify which elements of the business or technology may need to be rearchitected to deliver end-to-end resilience. As noted, the organization will already be providing many good things, and it is essential to reflect on how each element contributes to the program's overall success.

- Establishing a balance between productivity and resilience encourages people to be bold and innovate without unnecessary risk. The aim is to help, not hinder, the organization and to provide confidence in all that is to come.

We have now reached the end of the A-Z. I shall now be considering some final thoughts and reflections in the subsequent chapter.

CHAPTER 28
Final Thoughts

"Never underestimate your power to change yourself, never overestimate your power to change others."

— Dr. Wayner Dyer, U.S. Psychologist & Author

I want to leave you with concluding thoughts on building effective crisis management and resilience.

You will note that much of this book does not discuss the practical steps of creating and enacting an incident response plan but delves into deeper considerations that will influence your strategy and plan at a higher level.

I could tell you how to create a crisis management plan that looks pretty and covers all the things that auditors may be looking for. However, as we have concluded, a crisis is not pretty and, at times, will test your judgment in ways you may not expect. In some ways, you need to have lived and breathed some of these issues to know what works and what does not.

So here I am, sharing what I have learned along the way and what I continue to learn every day.

At the time of publication, my career has pivoted over 25 years – from starting in fraud and pivoting to business continuity, disaster recovery, cybersecurity, data protection, and privacy. Each of these falls under the broader banner of resilience, and each of these areas is underpinned by the need for effective crisis management.

A substantial portion of this book is deliberately centered on people. Never lose sight of what you are trying to protect. Even when my role was solely focused on the management and recovery of technology systems, it always served me to revert to my business continuity skills when considering what those technology systems were hosting, who are the users of those systems, and what the impact was as if they are not available. I have always been driven to consider the *'big picture.'*

I have come to the belief that sharing and collaboration are vital. Whether that is the good, the bad, or the downright ugly. A lesson shared is a problem halved; hence, I hope that sharing some of my experiences and stories will help and guide your path.

There will always be major events, some of which will test our resolve and some of which will cause us to dig deep. Still, despite everything, we have considerable opportunities to collectively make a difference in the lives of everyone now and into the future. This requires a commitment to providing a positive social impact for current and future generations to enable prosperity.

Now, I want to end where I started with *'Action.'*

Take a final moment for a final reflection to decide what action you will take as a result of reading this book. If there is one thing that has made you rethink the future to enable positive change, then this book has had the desired effect.

Some of the tasks may seem overwhelming, but these are not for you to bear alone. Do not underestimate how the strength of character and the tenacity to make a difference can cause a ripple effect amongst others. While a cultural shift can be complex and take time, seeing is believing, and people will follow your lead and action.

Building effective crisis management transcends organizations. In the spirit of sharing knowledge and building resilience,. if you have liked or learned one thing, please pass it on! We have our most positive impact when we can inspire others to act.

Index

A

action plan
  building 10
actions
  accountability, establishing 8, 9
  decision makers, assigning 9
  implementing 9, 10
assumptions
  removing 10, 11

B

believability
  establishing 16, 17
  versus, honesty 59
black swan event
  fallacy 101, 102
black swan events 2
Business Continuity (BC) 3

C

cause and effect
  correlating 193
communication
  case study 21-23
  method 25
  providing 24, 25
  stakeholder communications,
      tailoring 24
  stakeholders 25, 26
  verifying 26, 27
components
  breaking down 4
crisis 5
critical infrastructure 3

D

deep analysis
  performing 192, 193

deepfakes 45

digital disruption 2, 3

digital forensics 49

  considerations 50

diligence

  duty of care, establishing 31, 32

  in crisis 32

  risks, oversight 31

  tick-boxing, for compliance 33, 34

Disaster Recovery (DR) 3

disinformation 45

E

empathy

  demonstrating, for organizations 40

  demonstrating, for people 39, 40

  perils, of victim blaming 38, 39

F

facts

  checking 48, 49

  digital forensics 49, 50

  disinformation campaigns,
      impact of 46-48

  misinformation, versus
      disinformation 45

fake news 45

G

gravitas 54, 55

  demonstrating 55

H

honesty

  demonstrating 59

  grievances, dealing with 60, 61

  versus, believability 59

  whistleblowing, dealing with 60

I

incident

  versus crisis 4, 5

internet of everything 200

investigation

  case study 66-71

  co-ordinating 64, 65

  public inquiries, learning from 65, 66

  results 72

J

justice

  blame, apportioning 76, 77

  case study 78-87

  miscarriages 87

  negligence, dealing with 77, 78

K

knowledge

  awareness 94

  case study 91-94

  collaboration 94-96

  education 94

  sharing 94-96

  turning, into intelligence 90, 91

L

lessons

  applying 107

  case study 102-106

  fallacy, of black swan events 101, 102

  foresight, utilizing 100, 101

  hindsight, utilizing 100, 101

  isomorphic learning, importance 106,
      107

M

media

censorship, dealing with 112, 113

communicating with 111, 112

reliance, in crisis 110, 111

misinformation 45

multiple lines of inquiry

establishing 193

N

near misses 116

incident containment 117

O

opportunity

beyond comfort zone 120

leap of faith 121-123

negatives, turning into positives 127

pivoting, into crisis

management 125, 126

seismic change,

encountering 123-125

organizational resilience

demonstrating 144-146

P

people

importance 130, 131

over profit 131, 132

unpredictability 132, 133

Q

questions

during incident 137, 138

for post incident 138

for pre-incident 136, 137

R

resilience

culture and security,

embracing 143, 144

future-proofing resilience 142, 143

organizational resilience 144

strengthening 146

S

societal disruption 3

strategy

and culture 150

crisis response, exercising 152, 153

scenarios, developing 151

T

time

future 158

of essence 156

past 157

present 157

timeline

establishing, by retracing steps 188

trust

building 17

U

underdog

case study 162, 163

disrupter 163, 164

survival of fittest 163

University of Illinois Chicago (UIC)

law 32

V

victory

castle, protecting 168, 169

human needs 169, 170

positive reinforcement 170, 171

W

wellbeing
  case study 176-180
  emotional resilience, establishing 176
  maintaining, in crisis 174, 175
  path, finding 181
  stressors, managing 175
  trauma, dealing 181-183
  trauma, recognizing in others 183, 184

X

X-mark the spot 188

Y

Y-why 192

Z

zero trust
  boundary of cybersecurity,
    crossing 200
  boundary of technology,
    crossing 200
  business perspective 199, 200
  principles 198, 199

Made in United States
North Haven, CT
19 April 2024

51532034R00128